CW00541843

# BR 4007

# Guide to Ship Firefighting

Supersedes BR 4007 *Guide to Ship Firefighting* 1988

*March 1992*                    *By command of the Defence Council*

**MINISTRY OF DEFENCE**
Directorate of Naval Warfare
D/DNW/NSAS/P4007/1

© *Crown copyright 1992*

Applications for reproduction should be made to HMSO

First published 1988
Third edition 1992

ISBN 0 11 772733 4

*The BR 2170 series of publications mentioned within this book is not available outside the MOD.*

# Foreword

This edition supersedes the 2nd edition 1988 (Blue cover) which should be destroyed.

*Guide to Ship Firefighting,* (BR 4007) is made available to all new entry personnel and to Officers and Ratings during their Pre-joining Training (PJT) Firefighting Course.

In addition copies will be held by HM Ships, Submarines and RFA's. These will be distributed to Messes and also held by Divisional Officers in order to ensure that all prospective readers will find a copy readily available.

The aim of this book is to provide, in and easily understood format, the knowledge of fire prevention and firefighting which is taught during a PJT Firefighting course.

*Everyone in the RN and RFA is a potential fire fighter* and, for the safety of their shipmates and the safety of their ship everyone *must be constantly aware of fire hazards and be prepared to deal, effectively, with and outbreak of fire.*

# Contents

# List of figures

# 1    Causes of Fire

**Nature of fire**

**0101.** Fuel heat and oxygen must be in contact before a fire can be started. These can be represented by the three sides of a triangle and a fire cannot start, or continue, if one of these is absent or removed.

**Figure 1.1  Fire triangle**

**0102.  Components of a fire**

a.    **Fuel.** Fuel can be solid or liquid, which, when heated gives off flammable vapours. Fuel can also be a gas which starts to burn when its ignition temperature is reached. Examples are, paper, wood. cardboard, paint, oils, acetylene, propane gas.

b.    **Heat.** Heat can be transferred by:

    (1)    Radiation from any heating appliance, flames or explosion;

    (2)    *Conduction* through any suitable material such as steel or aluminium, decks or bulkheads; or

    (3)    *Convection* via gases, liquids or hot air circulated through ventilation trunking, lift shafts, etc.

c.    **Oxygen.** A supply of this gas, which is essential for combustion to take place, is available in the air.

**0103.  Types of fire.**

a. The British Standard method of classifying fires is by the nature of the fuel involved and is as follows:

(1)  **Class A**   Involving solid materials usually of an organic nature.
(2)  **Class B**   Involving liquids or liquefiable solids.
(3)  **Class C**   Involving flammable gases.
(4)  **Class D**   Involving metals.

b.  Most shipboard fires involve a variety of fuels and these classifications are not always appropriate.  In order that the appropriate firefighting equipment is provided at the scene of the fire (SOF) and the appropriate drills are initiated shipboard fires are categorised as follows:

(1)  **Category A - Solid fuel fire.**  Wood paper, cardboard fabrics and many other similar materials.
(2)  **Category B - Oil fuel fires.**  Lubricating oil, hydraulic oil, kerosene, diesel, petrol, etc.
(3)  **Category C - Electrical fire.**  Electricity does not burn. However, when  the origin of a fire is electrical (usually a fault in a live circuit which has generated enough heat to ignite a combustible material) it is referred to as an *electrical fire* which is a warning to firefighters. They will then take the necessary measures to locate local circuits associated with any fire.  Any circuits/equipments which are not under local control must be referred to HQ1/SCC/MSB  for the necessary action. Once the necessary circuits have been isolated, the fire is fought with the techniques and equipment appropriate to the material on fire.

**0104. Principles of extinction.**

a.   By cooling - the burning material is cooled below its ignition temperature , usually using water.
b.   By smothering - by excluding oxygen (air) from the burning material usually using $CO_2$, steam or foam.
c.   By removal of the fuel - accomplished by the removal of the combustible material or turning off the liquid fuel supply.
d.   By disrupting the chemical reaction of the burning process - by using halon gas (BCF/BTM).

# 2 Fire prevention

**0201. Introduction.** Fires onboard can destroy accommodation, stores, equipment, lives, and in extreme cases, the ship. Firefighting onboard is difficult and beset with dangers. When good fire prevention drills are exercised by the *whole* ship's company these difficulties and hazards are greatly reduced and can be almost eliminated. If you want to keep your *home* intact, then avoid the hazards of fire onboard by putting the *aide-memoire* into practice - it is more convenient and less dangerous than fighting fires.

**0202. Fire Prevention - *aide memoire***
  a. All private electrical equipment onboard must be checked safe by the ME department and logged.

  b. Clothes and other flammables must be kept clear of electrical radiators, hot equipment and systems.

  c. Smoking should only take place in spaces, and only in situations, where it is safe to do so. *Do not smoke in bed.* Do not smoke when moving around the ship and especially when on rounds. Do not flick cigarette butts or pipe knockings over the ships side. All smoking materials must be extinguished and placed in a suitable container, e.g. steel gash bin.

  d. Messdecks are to be kept tidy with all personal gear stowed in the kit lockers, which should be securely closed.

  e. Electric irons and soldering irons are to be switched off when not in use, and are to be allowed to cool before being stowed away. These appliances *must not* be left unattended when they are switched on.

  f. All paints and painting materials are to be returned to the Paint Shop/store on completion of work in accordance with Ship's Standing Orders (SSO's).

  g. All other highly inflammable materials, such as solvent, aerosols, some adhesives and liquids, gases and petrol, are to be used in accordance with the manufactures instructions, or current MOD(N) instructions and when not required for immediate use, to have their containers sealed.  At the end of the working day, they are to be placed, and secured, in an authorized stowage in accordance with SSO's.

h. All rags, especially wet or oily ones, sawdust and wood chips,etc., are to be safely disposed of at the end of the working day in accordance with the SSO's.

i. Spillages of oil, paint, solvents, spirits or other inflammable liquids are to be wiped up immediately and the dirty rags disposed of in accordance with SSO's.

j. When any compartment is vacated all unnecessary lighting and other electrical circuits are to be switched off.  The door to any empty compartment should, wherever possible, be kept shut.

k. The Welding Burning and Flame Heating Control Organization controls the safety/fire prevention aspects of all such operations (*see* BR 2170 Volume 1, Annex 22D).

l. Only safety matches are to be used onboard.

m. The use of single action cigarette lighters and the stowage of lighter fuels (petrol or butane gas) in kit lockers is not good fire prevention practice, and is to be discouraged.

n. When not in use all cleaning gear should be stowed in approved cleaning gear stowages.

o. On completion of the working day all gash bins from living spaces and waste bins from workshops must be emptied, and the waste disposed of in a safe manner.  It is recommended that gash bins and spitkids in living spaces should again be emptied before 'pipe down'.

p. When in harbour, inform the OOD immediately if any quantities of oil, or other flammable liquids, are observed overside so that action can be initiated for its safe and timely removal.  This is most likely to occur when your own or nearby ships are fuelling.

q. When not in use, TV sets, radios, record players, electric fans and other similar appliances are to be switched off and disconnected from the power source. Care must be taken not to obstruct ventilation with such appliances.

r.   On completion of work all papers, packs and books should be stowed in drawers, lockers or other approved stowages.

s.   When *No Smoking* is piped, or *No Smoking* signs are posted in an area or space - **DO NOT SMOKE!**

t.   When carrying out rounds be observant and report suspicious smells; leaks from any pipes or tanks; any electrical machinery that appears to be overheating and any wrongly stowed flammables. Check for irregular stowage spaces, masts, auxiliary machinery and other similar spaces. Report any safety/firefighting equipment that is missing or incorrectly stowed.

# 3  What to do on finding a fire

## Raise the alarm!

**Figure 3.1  Raising the alarm**

0301.  Raise the alarm with loud shouts of **'FIRE FIRE FIRE'**, giving the location of the fire.  If a ships internal telephone is at hand dial HQ1/QM (999) and report the fire giving the location, size and type of fire, details of any casualties and your name, as the person who found the fire

0302.  **If the fire is behind closed doors.**  If smoke is seen coming from behind a closed door it gives no indication as to the size or type of fire behind it.  *Do not tackle.*  Obtain fire fighting equipment in preparation for fighting the fire.  Brief the attack party leader and the report to the OOD in HQ1/SCC.

0303.  **If the door of the compartment on fire is open.** Raise the alarm as illustrated above and then carry on as follows:

    a.  If you are fully clothed attack the fire using first aid appliances appropriate to the type of fire.  Remember, *keep low* and make sure you have a safe line of retreat.  Brief the attack party leader and then report to the OOD in HQ1/SCC.

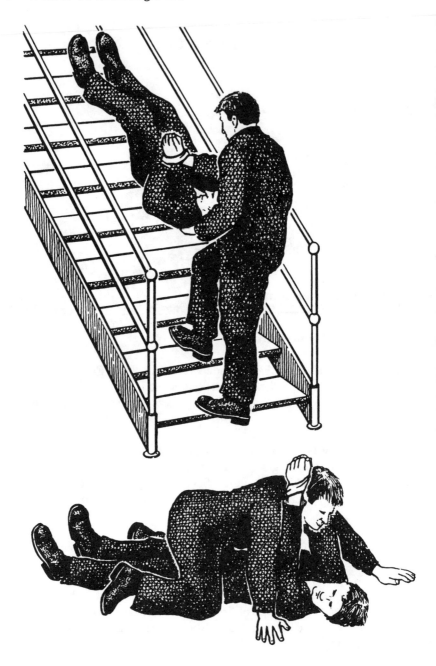

**Figure 3.2  Moving a Casualty**

b.  If, after your initial attack you are beaten back *close the door to the space* and start preparing hoses etc., as appropriate, ready for the attack party. Brief the attack party leader and then report to the OOD in HQ1/SCC.

c.  Move casualties to a safer place clear of the firefighting.

d.  Consider whether the fire can be prevented from spreading. If possible carry out appropriate action to contain. This can be achieved by cooling the boundary of the fire; removing flammable articles from the path of the fire; stopping local ventilation and switching off local electrical circuits.

e.  Stay in the vicinity of the fire ready to brief whoever is in charge, as follows:

   (1)  where the fire is situated;

   (2)  what is burning;

   (3)  any hazardous circumstances;

   (4)  position(s) and number(s) of casualties;

   (5)  achievements regarding the preparations for fighting the fire, e.g. boundary cooling, equipment to hand or rigged etc,: and

   (6)  details of electrical circuits and of any local ventilation fans which have been switched off.

f.  On completion of e. above go to HQ1/SCC and brief the OOD or senior rating in charge.

# 4    Firefighting organization

Introduction

**0401.** A fire can occur at anytime during a ship's service - in harbour or at sea - in peacetime or in wartime. The organization developed to deal with such a situation is explained in this chapter.

**0402.** A ship's organization and firefighting procedures must be capable of dealing with the worst possible case - a major fire when only a minimum number of hands are available to deal with it.

**Standard Harbour fire organization**
**0403.** The duty part of the watch in harbour (whether alongside, outside a Fleet base or at anchor) is the smallest unit that might be required to fight a major outbreak of fire. Therefore, this body of men must be organized to provide the following:

- **Specialist personnel** to maintain overall control of the incident and safety of the ship.

- **A main group** to locate, control and extinguish the fire as quickly as possible.

- **A containment party** to establish the boundaries of the fire and to contain it.

**0404.** The number of hands in each group, detailed in the following paragraphs, are the recommended minimum (based on the complement of a fully manned frigate). If they cannot be met the risk of ineffective firefighting will be increased. Whenever it is necessary to make reductions in numbers it is most important to retain the overall concept of the organization.

**0405.** To promote the effectiveness of this fire and emergency party the following actions are recommended:

a.   Daily orders should include the names of all members of the fire and emergency party and detail their specific duties within the organization.

b. At the forenoon muster of the fire and emergency party, or on taking over the duty, all the members are to be fully briefed on their individual tasks and responsibilities. It is too late to attend to these arrangements once an emergency has arisen.

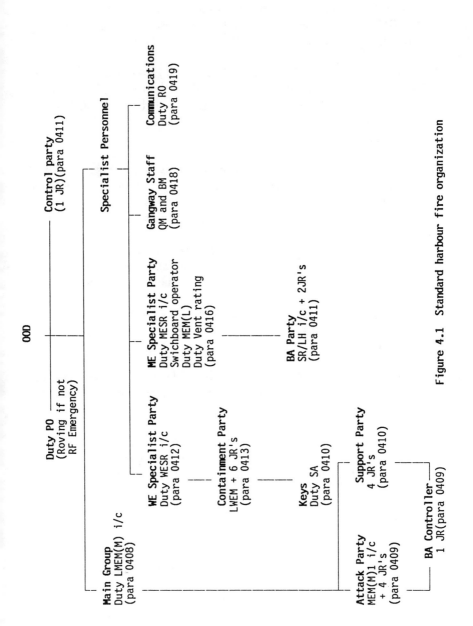

Figure 4.1  Standard harbour fire organization

## Notes

1. The **main group** should be under the overall charge of the Duty LMEM(M) who must have a thorough knowledge of the ship and firefighting techniques.

2. **The attack party** consists of an MEM(M)1 in charge plus at least one other MEM(M), one WEM, one Operations Department junior rating and one other JR. They are to be dressed in basic firefighting rig throughout the period of their duty. Two members of the attack party are to be BA wearers dressed in basic firefighting rig and BA.

3. The **support party** should consist of all those MEMs not specifically detailed  for either the attack party or the ME specialist party and should be under the charge of the 2nd duty MESR (No 3 of the firefighting team) or, if he is not available, a suitably experienced MEM.

4. The rating in charge of the **breathing apparatus party** is the BA co-ordinator and must be specifically trained in this task. All members of this party must be familiar with BA control and recharging techniques.

5. The **containment party** is to be led by the Duty LWEM. He is to liaise directly with the Duty WESR who is to be the containment co-ordinator within the control group at HQ1.

6. The Duty LWEM will also will also provide immediate guidance on electrical and electronic safety  and implement technical advice from the Duty WESR.

7. The containment party should contain all other duty personnel who have not been detailed for  other specific fire and emergency tasks.  Special duties ratings such as cooks, stewards and flight deck ratings should not be forgotten.

8. In the full harbour situation all ships should employ an ME senior rating and a separate qualified switchboard operator.

9. When wearing BASCCA men with beards experience up to 10% reduction in wear time due to the reduced efficiency of the face seal. Where practicable, in peacetime, men with beards should not be allocated duties which require them to wear BA. (In wartime all beards will have been shaved off.)

**0406. First aid firefighters.** These are the people who discover a fire and then carry out the drill in Chapter 3, *What to do on finding a fire.* **Remember** the person that found the fire must be sent to HQ1 for as soon as they can be spared or when ordered by the OOD.

## Main Group

**0407.** The precise function of the main group may alter depending upon the situation and nature of the fire, but the basic philosophy remains the same - the attack party must always be prepared to attack a fire **immediately** it is reported and the remainder of the group then maintains this attack **continuously** and **aggressively.** The main group is led by the Duty LMEM(M) who is identified by wearing a red and white striped surcoat.

**0408. Duty LMEM(M) Guidelines and Instructions.**

a.    He should have read and understood the following publications:

   (1)  BR 2170 Volume 1, Chapters 22 and 23.

   (2)  Ship's Standing orders,          Individual ships
        Chapter 15.                       may differ as to
                                          where the
                                          details of their
   (3)  Ship's NBCD Standing              firefighting
        Orders.                           orders and
                                          instructions are
                                          laid down

   (4)  Harbour Fire Exercise Assessment Form (paying particular attention to Umpire 1 section).

b.    On taking up his duty he is to muster the duty watch to ensure that they are aware of their tasks and responsibilities within the fire and emergency party organization.

c.    On hearing the alarm he should proceed immediately to a safe position as close as possible to the scene of the fire, in order to appraise the situation and to ensure that an effective initial attack is being made on the fire. With this first hand knowledge, and after debriefing the person who found the fire, he will be able to decide where to position himself and where to establish, after consultation with the DWESR, the smoke boundary.

d.  He must advise HQ1 when the fixed firefighting systems should be used (*see* BR 2170(1) paragraphs 2231/2 and Annex 22C-25/6).

c   He must also bear in mind that the attack BA men:

(1)  Should be dressed in overalls/No.8 working dress with sleeves rolled down

(2)  Should carry out the 10 second face seal check before entering the fire zone.

(3)  Will not necessarily be relieved by the four man firefighting team as they may have either put the fire out, run out of air or been beaten back by the fire.

(4)  Will have been nominated at the duty watch muster so that the BA Controllers' boards (Form S3047) can be made up in advance. (In making up the boards it is to be assumed that the pressure in each BA is 180 bar, and the time started to breathe taken as time the incident was piped.)

(5)  May be compelled, for any of a variety of reasons, to withdraw from their attack on the fire. Should this happen they must ensure that the compartment is sealed by shutting the hatch or door. Consideration should may also be given to holding the hatch or door on a waterwall, if circumstances permit.

f.  The Duty LMEM(M) must ascertain if there are any men trapped in the fire zone and if there are any injured men who require assistance.

g.  On the withdrawal of the attack BA men, the Duty LMEM(M) must ensure that the used firefighting appliances are moved out of the area from which the next attack is to be mounted.

h.  He must request, from HQ1, information on any specific hazards existing in the compartment on fire or in adjacent compartments. This information is included on form S3021, Compartment Firefighting check off cards, which are held at HQ1.

i.  He must supervise hose running, detailing the lengths of hoses required and the type of nozzles to be used. He should be guided by the following principles:

   (1) Firefighting hoses must be run from separate hydrants though it is acceptable to use a **Y** piece to supply a boundary cooling hose and a firefighting hose from the same hydrant.

   (2) Sufficient hose must be provided to allow the firefighters to reach all parts of a compartment.

   (3) Jet/spray nozzles have been renamed waterwall nozzles and spray/jet nozzles renamed firefighter nozzles. The firefighter nozzle has a considerably lower discharge rate than the waterwall nozzle and is therefore the preferred nozzle for firefighting between decks.

   (4) Waterwall nozzles must always be used to provide the waterwall, and the fire fighting nozzle is used for fighting carbonaceous fires.

j.  He must establish the nature of the fire and if there is a possibility that it is a fuel/oil fire he must ensure:

   (1) The firefighting medium is AFFF.

   (2) An FB5(X) branchpipe is used, in conjunction with a an inline inductor where appropriate.

   (3) Sufficient quantities of replenishment AFFF are provided for the support party. A 20 litre drum lasts approximately sixty seconds when supplying an FB5(X) branchpipe through a No.2 hose.

   (4) The number of drums to adequately blanket a compartment is shown adjacent to the foam inlet tube and this number should not be exceeded. It must be remembered that the foam will not spread evenly throughout a compartment owing to obstructions such as machinery, lockers, consoles etc., or if the ship has a heel.

k.  As soon as it is clear that the attack party is unable to extinguish the fire the Duty LMEM(M) must brief the four man team on the nature, location and size of the fire together with other useful information obtained from HQ1 and other sources, e.g., positions of hazardous items, such as, gas bottles, batteries etc. This briefing should take place in a suitable clean air environment where the team need not draw on air from their sets. He must ensure that each member of the team is conversant with his task within the team.

l.   The Duty LMEM(M) must ensure that all personnel not involved with a re-entry procedure are kept well clear of the door or hatch to be used. Having established this personnel boundary he must ensure that all those remaining in this area keep low to avoid any fireball

m.   As soon as the firefighting team has been deployed the Duty LMEM(M) must arrange, through the control team, for a relief team to be dressed and ready for briefing well before the team tackling the fire is due out.

n.   He will debrief all firefighting teams on their exit from the fire zone.

o.   He must keep the control team informed of the current situation especially when it is changing, for better or for worse. In the latter situation requests for additional manpower should be made early.

p.   The Duty LMEM(M) must continue to direct the main group's attack on the fire until he is sure  that the Local Authority Fire Brigade (LAFB)(which should arrive at the scene of the fire (SOF) quickly in the UK, and probably less quickly in some other parts of the world) is ready in all respects to commence firefighting,and has been fully briefed on taking over the firefighting task. He remains at the SOF and:

(1)   Liaises with the LAFB.

(2)   Maintains control over RN personnel who are assisting the LAFB in carrying out other firefighting tasks.

(3)   Keeps the OOD informed of the current situation and so assist him in his overall ship safety function.

**0409.   The attack party** consists of an MEM(M)1 in charge plus four other junior ratings all of whom are to be dressed in basic firefighting rig  - No.8

working dress or cotton overalls, woollen socks, DMS boots and red surcoats. Their aim is to attack the fire as quickly as possible.

a.  On the alarm being raised the MEM(M) plus two previously detailed junior rates are to attack the fire collecting SPE(AFFF) and CO2 fire extinguishers en route. They should establish the seat and nature of the fire using the Thermal Imaging Camera (TIC) if necessary

b.  The two men detailed as BA wearers, on hearing the alarm, are to don BA and proceed to attack the fire whether or not the BA Controller is present. The men being relieved (MEM(M) + 2) who are not wearing BA **must then withdraw** (see sub-paragraph d.) The effective use of BA will markedly improve the chances of maintaining a **continuous attack** on the fire.

c.  The BA controller will obtain his own BA control board (Form S3047) and enter on it the time of the fire pipe as the time of entry of the attack BA team.

d.  When relieved, or beaten back and their attack on the fire has to cease, the attack party is to join up with the support party and prepare for further firefighting.

### Notes

**1. Thermal Imaging Camera** (TIC). The prime use of the TIC is to locate the seat of the fire through smoke. It is also useful in search and rescue, identifying fuel leaks feeding a fire, locating firefighting equipment and spotting unexpected hazards in smoke logged areas. Until the arrival and involvement of the fearnought suitmen, the TIC is a valuable tool to the MEM(M) of the attack party. Initially the TIC is to be given to the MEM(M) i/c of the attack party by a member of the containment party (*see* paragraph **0412.b**). Subsequently its use will be controlled by the LMEM(M) i/c of the main group. In most circumstances where the TIC is needed the user will be wearing BA.

**2. Large compartments with more than one access point.** There is a risk that when the alarm is raised members of the attack party will proceed to differing access points and frustrate the aim of a co-ordinated attack. Provision is to be made in Ship's Orders for a standard muster point for each major space, so that these become well known and can also be piped when the initial alarm is raised. Simplicity is vital, therefore choice of port or starboard passage access to all compartments may be appropriate as standard operational procedure.

**3. BA Controllers.** All BA controllers are to be in possession of a watch for the period of their duty. There duties are:

> a.    To ensure that BA users are dressed correctly before entry to a fire.

> b.    To control BA users before entry to, and after exit from, a fire.

> c.    To be fully competent in the use of a BA control board, (*see* also paragraph **0716**), and the drill for BA face seal checks.

**0410. Support Party.** On the alarm being raised the support party is to muster, with all speed, at the designated FRPP. This party has two main tasks:

a.    To provide men dressed in full firefighting rig, (*see* paragraph **0703**), with a BA controller, to the scene of the fire as soon as possible.

b.    To co-ordinate, collect and provide to the SOF all necessary equipment to sustain a continuous attack on the fire (hoses, nozzles, inline inductors, AFFF, etc.). Manpower for the latter task is to be provided from those remaining in the support party when the first task is achieved, members of the retiring attack party and from supplementary personnel onboard when the alarm is raised,

Support party fearnoughtsuitmen are to be dressed in basic firefighting rig throughout the period of their duty. Surcoats are to be worn (*see* paragraph **0422**). On the alarm being sounded these men are to don anti-flash gloves and anti-flash hood, seamen's stockings, firefighting boots, fearnought suit and fearnought mittens, BA, bulb horn, protective helmet with portable radio communications set, (transceiver) and cap lamp as advised in paragraph **0424**. When fully dressed they are to be taken to the SOF by the BA controller and reported to the LMEM(M) i/c of the main group. The support party should be deployed, initially, as follows:

● No.1 - Waterwall operator.

- No.2 - Fire fighter with appropriate appliance, viz firefighter nozzle or FB5(X).

- No.3 - Thermal Imaging Camera operator (Leader).

- No.4 - Hose tender.

- BA controller.

## Control and Specialist parties

**0411. Control Party.** On the alarm being raised, the control rating is to close up in HQ1 (or another suitable position with adequate communications should it not be possible to occupy HQ1) and man the incident board and internal communication lines. He is to make a chronological record of events during the incident. The OOD must not become to involved in the details which are the responsibility of the ratings in charge of the various groups and parties, but he must consider the following:

a. The possible hazards from explosives and flammables.

b. The availability of equipment, power supplies, fire and salvage pumps.

c. The hazards of smoke and smoke clearance.

d. Safety of personnel, including any civilians who may be onboard.

e. Ship stability.

f. Control and Allocation of additional manpower.

g. Liaison with adjacent ships and outside authorities.

### Notes

1. Smoke clearance action must neither fan the fire nor smoke-log otherwise clear areas crucial to the firefighting task. There are two main methods of clearing smoke.

    a. Using large exhaust fans such as the galley and main machinery space fans to suck the smoke from the affected areas.

    b. Using large supply fans to build up a pressure to blow the smoke from the ship.

2. In both cases (Notes 1a and 1b above) there will normally be a need to open up an air route along which smoke can pass to atmosphere, or to facilitate the required air flow to achieve effective smoke clearance.

3. Smoke control and clearance exercises should be practised regularly so that the necessary personnel are made familiar with the arrangements and equipment fitted.

**0412. WE Specialist.** On the alarm being raised, the duty WE Senior Rate is to close up in HQ1. He is responsible for:

a. Ensuring firefighting teams have access to magazines in the vicinity of the fire.

b. Advising the OOD on the following:

    (1) Magazine and explosive safety.

    (2) Movement of ammunition.

    (3) Magazine fire fighting arrangements, spray systems and fitted pumping arrangements.

    (4) Electronic and electrical equipment safety.

    (5) Internal and external communications.

c. Acting as containment co-ordinator, liaising between the rating in charge of the containment party, specialist parties and the OOD, in order to establish priorities for the containment task and to ensure that the duties listed in paragraph **0413** are effectively executed.

**0413. Containment party.** On the alarm being raised, members of the containment party are to muster with all speed at a convenient point near to, but separate from, the support party. The location of the muster point must be included in the initial fire alarm broadcast. The duties of the containment party include:

a.  Establishing the immediate boundary of the fire by searching all adjacent compartments, lockers and stowages - not forgetting ventilation trunking to and from the affected area.

b.  Provision of a TIC to the SOF. A rating is to be predesignated to ensure this happens.

c.  Removing flammable materials from the vicinity of the fire boundary.

d.  Action to limit the spread of smoke and preparations for smoke removal. Specific instructions are to be obtained from HQ1 before affecting smoke removal measures.

e.  Rigging of boundary cooling, monitoring of bulkhead temperatures and provision of manpower to implement boundary cooling where necessary.

f.  Action to minimise the dangers to personnel from electrical equipments and to prevent, as far as possible, damage to electronic and electrical equipments from the effects of firefighting/boundary cooling water.

g.  Action to remove or drain down free surface water.

0414. The Duty LWEM, as leader of the containment party, is to be briefed by the Duty WESR on the location of all the adjacent compartments and to be made aware of those compartments presenting the greatest hazard, e.g., magazines, gas bottle stowages. fuels, flammables, etc. He should constantly check the boundaries to ensure that his team has contained the incident and is to keep the OOD informed through direct liaison with the DWESR. He is to provide first hand guidance on the safety of electronic and electrical equipment and personnel. Smoke control measures initiated by the attack party become the responsibility of the containment party once it has closed up. He is to initiate local smoke control measures, using ventilation, as directed by HQ1, and to report back on their effectiveness and the location of smoke boundaries.

**0415. Keys Rating.** On the alarm being raised, the rating responsible for keys is to obtain the keys to the duplicate keyboard from the OOD, and then provide to the ratings in charge of both main group and containment party the necessary keys to enable firefighters to gain access to all compartments in the vicinity of the fire

**0416. ME Specialist Party.** This party is responsible for:

a.  Maintaining the integrity of the ship's electrical power supplies and safeguarding those to electrical services, if necessary by shedding load and/or putting additional generators on load. Where possible, normal and alternative power supplies to the fire pumps should be established and maintained during firefighting operations.

b.  Crash stopping ventilation, shutting upper deck vent flaps on systems serving the compartment on fire, and subsequent operation of other vent systems for smoke clearance.

c.  Checking all fire pumps and starting additional pumps to maintain the high pressure sea water (HPSW) system pressure. If necessary, this is to be achieved by shutting off sea water to non essential services.

d.  Isolating electrical power supplies in and around the area of the fire to minimize the danger to firefighters and equipments.

e.  Checking and safeguarding those systems essential to the firefighting effort (saturated steam, HP air, etc.) and isolating those systems containing hazardous fluids (fuel, lub oil, hydraulics, etc.) to prevent them from feeding the fire.

f.  Making contact and liaising with the shore electrical supply authority.

g.  Advising the OOD on fixed firefighting installations for machinery spaces, paint shop, flammable store rooms, gas bottle stowages, hangars, etc., and, if appropriate, starting auxiliary boilers to supply saturated steam.

h.  Advising the OOD on the following:

    (1)  The technical aspects of firefighting.

(2)  Pumping and salvage arrangements.

(3)  Ventilation and smoke clearance.

(4)  Ship stability.

(5)  The presence of compressed gases or pressure vessels in the vicinity of the fire, including HP air, refrigerant gases, oxygen and acetylene gases, beer kegs and associated $CO_2$ bottles.

(6)  The nature of the ship's structure, i.e., aluminium or steel on the area of the fire.

**0417. Breathing apparatus party.** On the alarm being raised the BA co-ordinator organizes his party to collect BA and spare cylinders to form a dump in a position allowing room to work and free from smoke. This location is to be broadcast. Once the necessary BA has been collected (excluding the 4 designated for the upper deck re-entry locker) the party becomes responsible for:

a.  Provision of BA to required user locations.

b.  Recharging used BA cylinders.

c.  Informing the OOD of the BA availability state. [Using the BA Coordination (Tote) Board.]

d.  Co-coordinate optimum use of BA procured from outside sources (other ships etc.).

e.  Provision and briefing of other BA controllers other than BA controllers pre-designated as members of the main group. (*see* Note 2 below).

### Notes

1.  Both the BA co-ordinators and the ratings detailed to recharge cylinders are to be trained in recharging techniques.

2.  BA Controllers in the main group (*attack and support parties*) are not members of the BA party as such. The BA co-ordinator is

responsible that all men detailed for BA control duties are fully briefed at the start of their period of duty.

3.    Careful consideration must be given to the location of the initial, and other BA dumps. Ideally, when smoke logging dictates the need to move the dump away from the vicinity of the activated FRP an alterative position should be selected on the upper deck to SOF guideline route. This ensures that personnel wearing BA will be able to locate the BA dump easily on withdrawal and that the ship's and the LAFB dumps can be collocated. As standard operating procedure (SOP) the LAFB set up their BA dump on the upper deck to SOF guideline route.

4.    Fire produces formidable smoke and toxic fume hazards. BA co-ordination and BA wearer control are essential and vital parts of the firefighting organization and must be practised regularly.

**0418. Gangway Staff.** On receipt of the fire alarm, from whatever source, a pipe is to be made by the gangway staff or HQ1/SCC watchkeeper, as appropriate, informing the ship's company of the existence of a fire, its location and where various members of the fire and emergency party are to muster - this pipe is to be repeated. When available the main broadcast alarm is to be used prior to making this initial emergency broadcast. Thereafter the gangway staff or the HQ1 watchkeeper (depending on access to shore telephone) are to carry out the following.

a.    Inform the Local Authority Fire Brigade (LAFB).

b.    Inform shore authorities.

c.    Inform adjacent ships.

d.    If the LAFB has arrived then once the appropriate route to the SOF from the ON brow has been agreed between the officer responsible for ship safety and the LAFB officer the ships staff are to identify the route by running a combined guide and sound powered telephone line.

e.    Control entry to and exit from the ship.

f.    Prepare to meet the LAFB Officers and escort them to HQ1/OOD.

g.  Keep a red flag in daytime, or a red light at night at the foot of the ON brow.

**0419. Communications Rating.** On the alarm being raised, a Duty RO is to carry out the following tasks:

a.  Rig a sound powered telephone between HQ1 (or other control position) and the SOF.

b.  Man emergency communications nets to outside authorities.

### Notes

1.  Task a. above should be undertaken by the HQ1 incident board operator/communications number when in the reduced harbour fire party organization.

2.  Task b. is only to be undertaken when the full fire party organization is in force and there are two duty RO's in the duty watch.

## Emergencies

**0420.** As soon as it becomes apparent that a fire is more than a minor incident, the OOD should not hesitate to declare a full scale emergency. It will ensure that all uninvolved personnel are brought out of the ship and clear of danger. It will also provide a ready pool of spare hands for extra fire fighting and containment tasks. The correct pipe for initiating an emergency is: '**Emergency, Emergency, Emergency, Clear lower deck of all personnel not involved in firefighting, muster on the ..... keeping clear of the fire area**'. ( ..... pipe should give the appropriate muster point bearing in mind the weather, do not always use the flightdeck as a matter of course). This broadcast should be prefixed by the use of the main broadcast alarm.

## Personnel Safety and Control

**0421.** In the event of a full scale emergency being declared, it is important that every person onboard (including civilian personnel where appropriate) can be accounted for as quickly as possible. Ratings in charge of the various duty groups and parties should account for their personnel and report to the OOD. Departmental nominal lists should be compared with leave boards/cards to ascertain the names of those who should be onboard and an officer or rating should be nominated from available personnel to muster non duty personnel and report back to the OOD.

## Identification of personnel (Fire and Emergency party)

0422. In order to facilitate the easy recognition of fire and emergency party personnel coloured surcoats should be worn as follows:

- Red and white stripes - rating i/c main group.

- Red - Main group with the exception of the BA controller.

- Yellow - BA party, plus the BA controllers of the attack party and the support party.

## Use of improved firefighting communication system

0423.   Five portable radio transmitter/receivers (transceivers) will be available in most ships, at each FRPP. Each set consists of a lightweight protective helmet (Slim Tank Helmet (STH)) including microphone and earphones, the portable transceiver and press to transmit switch.

0424. These sets are deployed as follows:

- Support party fearnought suitman No.1 (waterwall).

- Support party fearnought suitman No.2 (firefighter).

- Support party fearnought suitman No.3 (TIC and leader)

- Support party fearnought suitman No.4 (hose tender)

- Rating i/c main group (provided by support party BA controller)

- The remaining sets are for use by the reliefs of Nos.1, 2, 3 and 4 and one spare.

0425 - 0430.  Spare

# Reduced harbour fire organization

**0431.** When a ship is in a Fleet base, and expert firefighting assistance is readily available from its LAFB, the size of the fire and emergency party may be reduced, but not in the specialist parties, in whose duties the LAFB are not trained. In some ships, the availability of Deterrence and Response Forces (D&RF) trained manpower, particularly junior ratings, may not permit the Attack Party to be divorced from security duties. If unavoidable, this can be accepted but only in the reduced harbour fire organisation.

**0432.** This reduced organization is independent of the Notice for Sea and represents the minimum number of people who can be retained onboard whenever a ship is operational. It should not be further reduced. However, when ships are working a dormant leave routine, the fire and emergency party can cover more than one ship and its numbers can be found from the total duty personnel of *paired* ships.

**0433.** When a ship is non operational the problems are somewhat different and the composition of the fire and emergency party when the ship is in refit is not covered here. (Note:    Ships in DED are usually still operational). However, when the composition of a fire and emergency party is less than twenty the following guidelines apply:

a.    The OOD's position and fire dump is to be established in a specified area, e.g., the hangar.

b.    An attack party with ratings detailed to wear BA is nominated, and they must be prepared to don full Fearnought if the need arises.

c.    Any additional personnel on board must form a containment party.

### Notes

1.    The attack party under the leadership of an MEM(M)1 should contain at least one other MEM(M), one WEM, one Operations Department junior rating and one other JR. They are to be dressed in basic firefighting rig throughout the period of their duty.

2.    The four members of the support party are to dress in full firefighting rig and BA before reporting to the rating in charge of the main group. The attack party BA controller is to act as controller for all members of the main group.

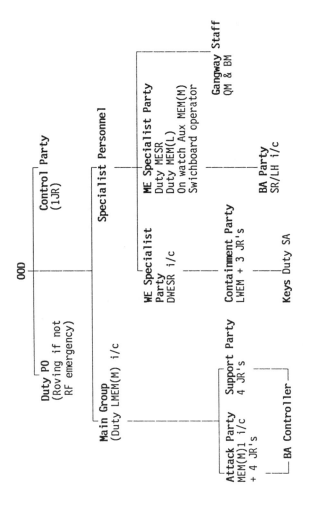

Figure 4.2 Reduced fire party organization

3.    In addition to taking charge of the containment party the LWEM should also provide guidance on electronic and electrical safety.

4.    The containment party should contain all other duty personnel who have not been detailed for other specific fire and emergency party tasks.  Special duties ratings such as cooks, stewards and flight ratings should not be forgotten.

5.    The on watch Bosun's Mate may run out the guideline from the gangway to the SOF.

6.    The duty SA is to act as a member of the containment party once he has obtained the keys for all compartments in the fire area.

7.    Provided he is suitably qualified, the duty ME senior rate may, in ships where the main switchboard and HQ1 are co-located, also undertake the duties of switchboard operator.

## Firefighting at sea - standing sea fire party (SSFP)

0434.  In all ships at sea there must be a party of specifically detailed firefighters under the charge of a suitable senior rating, which is available at all times and ready for an immediate response to a fire.  The party should be made up from daywork personnel.

### Organization

0435.  The Standing Sea Fire Party (SSFP) should comprise all the firefighting groups and parties detailed in the previous paragraphs (main, containment and specialist), when daywork manpower is readily available.

0436.  In smaller ships the number of daywork hands available to form the SSFP is likely to be more limited and therefore, in frigates and destroyers, the suggested minimum requirement is for an attack party comprising one senior rating in charge of six junior ratings and, in addition, the necessary control personnel.  All the ratings should be daywork personnel and the aim should be to achieve continuity and a well trained team.  Although the actual composition of this party is at the Commanding Officers discretion, the most suitable attack party senior rating is probably the CMEM(M).  The junior ratings should ideally be drawn from all departments and one should be from the ventilation party. They should not be detailed as special sea dutymen.

**0437.** In ships smaller than a frigate, or those where daywork manpower is very restricted, the size of the SSFP may need to be further reduced. If this is the case, the concept of the attack party should still be retained. For example, where there are only four junior ratings available to form the attack element, two are to don BA.

**0438. Emergency stations.** If the SSFP is unable to cope with a fire, either due to lack of personnel or shortage of material resources, it is important that the ship be piped to emergency station in good time. This will get the right people to the right places quickly and bring the ship's fire and repair parties to State 1. It will also clear the area of unwanted personnel, allow off watch watchkeepers to be accounted for and provide back-up where necessary. The actual stage at which the ship should be piped to emergency stations will obviously vary depending upon the size of the SSFP and the rate of escalation of the incident.

**Identification of personnel (Standing Sea Fire Party)**

**0439.** In order to facilitate the identification of SSFP personnel coloured surcoats should be worn as follows:

● Red and white stripes - Senior rating when i/c of the SSFP.

● Red - Attack party and main groups of ships larger than DD/FF with the exception of BA controllers.

● Yellow - BA party, plus the attack party and support party BA controllers.

**Procedure**

**0440.** In ships larger than destroyers or frigates where the SSFP comprises all the firefighting groups and parties of the full harbour organization, the procedure to be followed is much the same as when the ship is in harbour.

**0441.** When the alarm is raised in a ship with only an attack party of six junior ratings, the rating in charge and three others should proceed directly to the SOF. They are to collect portable first-aid firefighting appliances and the TIC en route, and join up with such firefighters as there may be.

Having established the seat and nature of the fire, they are to fight it with the appropriate appliances. The two ratings detailed as BA men are to don their sets and proceed to attack the fire whether or not the BA Controller is present. The men being relieved, who are not wearing BA, *must then withdraw*. The BA Controller will obtain his own control board and enter on it the time of the fire pipe as the time of entry of the attack BA men and a pressure of BA as 180 bar. All members of the attack party are to be fully experienced in dressing and wearing BA as well as being capable of using a control board.

**0442.** In those ships with numbers other than six junior ratings in the attack party the firefighting procedure should be adjusted to suit the numbers involved.

**0443.** As soon as the initial alarm is raised, HQ1 should be manned by the Action NBCD Officer, an incident board operator, a communications number and the Explosives Safety Officer (ESO); Switchboards should be manned by qualified switchboard operators to crash stop ventilation and to safeguard electrical supplies; SCC/MCR/ER watchkeepers should put all available fire pumps on to the HPSW systems. The first task of the communications number is to rig a sound powered telephone between the control position and the SOF.

**0444.** The Executive Officer should briefly visit the SOF and HQ1 in the early stages, in order to gain an up to the minute appreciation of the situation so that he will be able to give advice to the Command on whether there is a need for the ship to go to emergency stations.

**First aid firefighting during silent hours**

**0445.** It is recommended that the following on-watch ratings be detailed to undertake first aid firefighting until relieved by the SSFP; an MEM, an RO, a Bosun's Mate and an Operations Department rating either from the Operations room or the watch on deck.

**0446 - 0450.** Spare.

## Firefighting in conjunction with Local Authority Fire Brigades

### Liaison

**0451.** A good liaison with Local Authority Fire Brigades (LAFBs) is essential if efficient use is to be made of their service in the event of fire. This liaison is vital when a ship is in harbour for any length of tine and the ship's company is depleted (e.g. By leave or training).

**0452.** Contact with the LAFB in a home Naval Base should be made, in the first instance, through the Ministry of Defence Area Fire Prevention Officer (AFPO). The AFPO should be kept up to date with any significant changes that might affect the ship's firefighting capability, e. g., docking, leave period, supply of additional pumps, etc. The AFPO or one of his officers will attend ships fires during normal working hours, but this attendance may be delayed during silent hours. It is therefore most important to establish a direct liaison with the LAFB.

**0453.** Successful liaison with the LAFB depends upon an understanding of any differences in aims between the RN and LAFB.

**0454.** The firefighting priorities of the LAFB are as follows:

a.    To save life.

b.    To save property.

c.    To extinguish the fire.

**455.**    a. Ships standing orders are to contain instructions for calling the LAFB as an automatic response to the discovery of a suspected or known fire when a ship or submarine is berthed in a Naval Base, commercial port or shipyard. At anchor or at a buoy this assistance should be considered at an early stage, paying due regard for the ships geographical location and the probability of useful and timely assistance from local authorities.

b. Upon arrival of the LAFB senior fire office attending the incident is to be met at the brow and escorted directly to the ship's officer responsible for the safety of the ship (Officer of the Day (OOD) for

RN ships or submarines, Duty deck Officer for the RFA). At this stage the LAFB may establish a Control Point (CP), an Advanced Control Point (ACP) and a breathing apparatus and firefighting equipment dump in the most appropriate locations. Should the LAFB subsequently become involved in the incident, communications are to be established between the officer responsible for ship safety and the LAFB Control Point and, whenever possible, an RN/RFA liaison officer or senior rating should be stationed at the LAFB Control Point.

c. The ship's officer responsible for the safety of the ship is to fully brief the senior fire officer on the situation, and then, after consultation with him, decide on the appropriate strategy to deal with the incident. Dependent on the nature of the incident and the ship's resources available to him the ship's officer responsible for ship safety may then request the LAFB to undertake some indeed all aspects of the operation. Any request for assistance should be clearly recorded. If LAFB assistance is accepted control of the firefighting aspects of the incident is to be given to the Senior Fire Brigade Officer.

d. The level of involvement of the LAFB will be determined by the operational state of the vessel and the ships complement. As a general rule frigates and above that are operational may require less assistance than minor war vessels or submarines. Due to limited manpower resources, RFAs and ships under repair will generally require major assistance from the LAFB. The initial level of attendance is predetermined by individual local authorities and will normally be in the order of 4 appliances.

## Ship Safety

**456.** Notwithstanding the involvement of the LAFB in some or all aspects of the operation the Commanding Officer, or his designated representative, retains full overall responsibility for all firefighting measures and the safety of the ship, but not the control of LAFB personnel if they are committed to the firefighting task. It is imperative that no matter what firefighting strategy is adopted, until such time that the fire is extinguished a continued attack on the fire is maintained.

**Jetty space**
0457. Wherever physical conditions permit, a clear space (7.5 m radius) should always be kept clear near the foot of the brow; LAFB appliances require a space 10.5 m by 5.0 m for parking and operation, although certain special appliances may require somewhat larger area. The area is to be conspicuously marked *Fire Brigade - Keep Clear*. The Naval Base authorities will provide assistance in the supply of suitable notices.

**Brows**
0458. When a ship has more than one brow a clear indication is to be given as to which one should be used by the LAFB officer to come aboard. A red flag should be used in the daytime and a red light at night, to mark the **ON** brow. The LAFB officer is to be met at the brow by an officer or senior rating with authority to answer his questions.

**Probable questions**
0459. The following are among the questions likely to be asked by the first senior LAFB officer to arrive at the scene:

a.    Is anyone missing and/or injured?

b.    Where is the fire?

c.    What is burning?

d.    Have electrical supplies to the ship/fire zone been isolated?

e.    How long have the fires been burning?

f.    How did the fire start?

g.    What action is being taken by ship's staff?

h.    What is the state of the ship's HPSW system?

i.    Are there any dangerous compartments adjacent?

j.    What is the state of the ship's fire and emergency party?

k.    How critical is the ship's stability?

l.    How much water has been pumped in?

m.  Are timber docking shores affected?

n.  Has a smoke boundary been set up? If so, where?

## Missing personnel

0460. The LAFB may well arrive before an accurate check has been made as to whether any personnel are unaccounted for.  During the initial consultations between the LAFB and the ship's officer in charge of firefighting a decision as to whether search and rescue operations by the LAFB are required in preference to firefighting assistance may well have to be made.

## Electrical supplies

0461. The LAFB normally expect all electrical supplies to an installation on fire to be isolated.  This is seldom practicable in a warship on fire.  However, when there is a risk of voltages in excess of 440 volts the equipment should be isolated.  It must be noted that attempts at maintaining a *keep alive* policy may be counter-productive when compared with the savings in damage through quick extinction of the fire (*see* paragraph **0412** which deals with boundary cooling and precautions concerning electrical equipment).

## Route to the fire

0462. Once the route to the fire from the **ON** brow has been agreed between the officer responsible for ship safety and the LAFB officer, the ship's staff are to identify the route by running a combined guide and sound powered telephone line.

## Control of Firefighting personnel

0463. Strict control over the combined numbers of personnel involved on the firefighting operation will need to be exercised and therefore, all RN/RFA personnel not directly involved must keep clear of the ship.  This will be achieved by sounding the main broadcast alarm and making the pipe "EMERGENCY, EMERGENCY, EMERGENCY, CLEAR LOWER DECK OF ALL NON DUTY PERSONNEL, MUSTER ON THE JETTY (or other nominated position) KEEPING CLEAR OF THE FIRE AREA". Entry and egress must be controlled by the gangway staff at the brows.

## Withdrawal of personnel

0465. If the LAFB is delegated the task of finding and/or fighting the fire, RN/RFA personnel will be gradually withdrawn from within the smoke boundary as they are replaced by LAFB personnel.  Ship's firefighters, working in pairs and wearing BA, will normally be required to act as guides. Close collaboration between the officer or rating in charge of the ship's main group and the LAFB officer at the ACP is essential.

**0466.** The officer or rating in charge of the ships main group, once relieved by the LAFB at the scene of the fire, is to move to the ACP. His duties will be:

a. to liaise with the LAFB officer in charge at that position;

b. to keep HQ1 informed of all actions being taken;

c. to maintain control of all the RN/RFA personnel actively engaged in firefighting (but see para. 0470)

**Evacuation of HQ1**

**0467.** Should HQ1 (or alternative position) need to be evacuated for any reason, it is recommended that the ship's control team moves to the brow nearest the LAFB control. If this is not practicable, any other location in clear air with good ship's internal communications should be selected (e.g. bridge wing).

**Communications**

**0468.** The ship is to provide a communication link from HQ1 (or alternative position) to the SOF, and from the brow to the SOF, manned by ships staff at both ends. LAFB officers will normally use their own communication systems, but these may prove inadequate in a war ship environment and, in some cases, the associated RADHAZ prohibits their use.

**Use of breathing apparatus and control**

**0469.** When the ship's firefighters are using BA, consideration should be given to establishing the BA co-ordinator at the ACP as soon as possible. The BA controllers (for members of the ship's fire party wearing BA) will then retreat up the guideline as the smoke boundary spreads. This will ensure that men wearing BA will find their controller when they leave the smoke boundary.

**0470.** Ship's staff BA controllers should continue to control ship's personnel using BA, at the same time maintaining the closest possible liaison with the LAFB controllers. Should firefighting measures be assigned to the LAFB, overall co-ordination of all BA wearers is to be exercised by the LAFB officer in charge of the firefighting operations.

**0471 -0474.**  Spare.

# Firefighting in wartime   (States 1 or 2)

**0475. Firefighting in state 1.** The local control of firefighting is undertaken by the FRP leader.   The four man firefighting team (dressed in full firefighting rig) are used as the support party for men in the fire zone already attacking the fire.   The remaining hands are used to form the relief firefighting team and in the BA support and containment roles.  Additional support can always be sought from other FRPs and other positions as detailed and co-ordinated by HQ1, who should respond in direct relation to the size of the fire, damage and associated problems. *See* Figures 4.3 and 4.4. for the organizational diagrams.

**Firefighting in state 2.**
**0476.**   All the positions shown in figs.4.3 and 4.4 are manned, but not necessarily by the personnel detailed in state 1.   When these positions are manned in state 2 it is referred to as being in Defence Watches, and the numbers of men so stationed will vary, according to the complement and other considerations, from ship to ship.   In the event of fire the men on watch attack it as detailed in chapter 3, the ship assuming State 1 immediately in order to get all the DC and FF personnel in position so that full firefighting teams can be organized and co-ordinated.

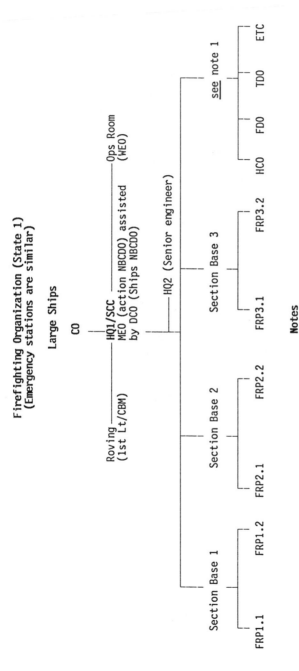

Firefighting Organization (State 1)
(Emergency stations are similar)

Large Ships

**Notes**

1. Areas of the ship concerned with specialized tasks, e.g., hangars, flight decks, tank decks, etc., are organized at section base level for control and reporting.

2. Rig for action stations; No 8s, DMS boots, anti-flash (hood and gloves) and action coveralls.

3. Each FRP details and dresses 4 men in full firefighting clothing, BA worn but unmasked, helmets to hand. Four other men are detailed as relief firefighters. Each team of four has a BA controller detailed.

Figure 4.3  Firefighting organization (State 1) - large ships

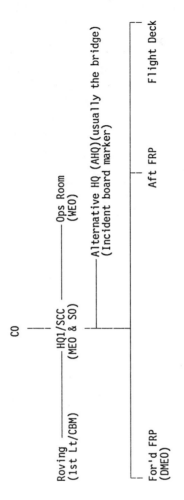

Firefighting organization (State 1)
(Emergency stations are similar)

Smaller Ships – DD/FF

CO

Roving ————— HQ1/SCC ————— Ops Room
(1st Lt/CBM)      (MEO & SO)            (WEO)

Alternative HQ (AHQ)(usually the bridge)
(Incident board marker)

For'd FRP          Aft FRP          Flight Deck
(DMEO)

**Notes**

1. Rig for action stations; No 8's, DMS boots, anti-flash(hood and gloves) and action coveralls.

2. Each FRP details and dresses 4 men in full firefighting clothing, BA worn but unmasked, helmets to hand. Four other men are detailed as relief firefighters. Each team of four has a BA controller detailed.

Figure 4.4  Firefighting organization (State 1) – Smaller ships

# 5   First aid firefighting equipment

## Portable fire extinguishers (first aid appliances)

**0501.**  9 litre stored pressure extinguisher (AFFF)
(SPE(AFFF))

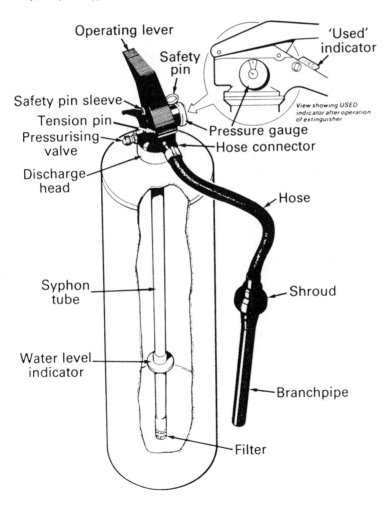

Fig. 5.1   9 litre stored pressure extinguisher(AFFF) - SPE(AFFF)

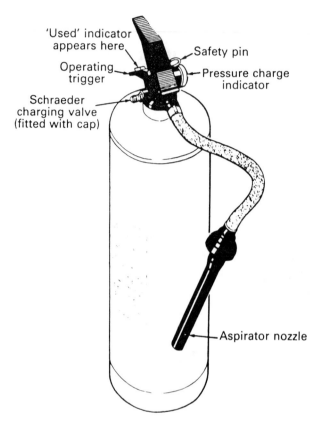

'Used' indicator appears here

Operating trigger

Schraeder charging valve (fitted with cap)

Safety pin

Pressure charge indicator

Aspirator nozzle

**Fig. 5.2    9 litre stored pressure extinguisher (AFFF) - SPE(AFFF)**

The discharge from this appliance can be controlled by means of the operating lever which can be released whilst it is being re-directed, thus preventing wastage. The appliance can be re-charged by means of either a portable compressed air bottle, a low pressure air line or a foot pump after it has been refilled as follows:

a.    Ensure that all pressure has been released and unscrew the discharge head assembly, complete with the syphon tube, and withdraw it from the shell.

b.    Wash out the inside of the shell thoroughly with fresh water.

c.    Pour 8.6 litres of clean, fresh water into the extinguisher using the syphon tube as a dipstick. The correct amount of water is indicated when it reaches the end of the syphon when the measuring shoulder, which projects out from the side of the syphon tube, is rested on the lip at the top of the extinguisher. Using a AFFF measuring cylinder (graduated, acrylic, 500 ml - from the fire locker) top up the extinguisher with 0.4 litres of AFFF thus making the contents 9 litres.

### Note

Should sea water ever be used to fill the extinguisher in an emergency, it is to be well rinsed out with clean fresh water after use, and before refilling and recharging.

d.  When the AFFF solution level is correct, replace the discharge head assembly and hand tighten.

### Note

A thin film of grease (Vaseline) is to be applied to the head seating 'O' ring before replacing the head assembly.

e.  Raise the operating lever to its non-operational position, insert the safety pin and retain it by fitting a Hellerman rubber sleeve to the end of the pin.

f.  Re-set the USED indicator.

g.  Remove the air charging valve dust cap and connect the compressed air supply to the charging valve.

h.  After charging (*see* paragraphs **0502, 0503 or 0504.**) disconnect the air supply and replace the dust cap. Release excess air as in the note with paragraph **0504.**

i.  With the SPE in the upright position check for signs of leakage around the cylinder head.

j.  With the nozzle housed stow and secure the SPE, using the arrangements provided.

**0502.   Pressurization arrangements - SPE(AFFF).**   Pressurization is normally carried out using the portable air charging assembly, the ship's breathing air charging panel or a foot pump. These systems are described below.

**0503.**   Where possible the SPE(AFFF)'s are to be charged to 10 bar - the working pressure - indicated within the black segment on the extinguisher pressure gauge. The performance of the SPE(AFFF) at 7 bar is, however, acceptable. Therefore when using a tyre pressure gauge and the foot pump, a 7 bar charge is acceptable although this will not indicate a full charge.

**0504.   Portable air charging assembly.**   This assembly   (*see* Figure 5.3) consists of a 1240 litre free air capacity steel high pressure air cylinder fitted with a regulator valve, pressure gauges and a discharge hose terminating in a connection which will mate with the air charging connection on the SPE. The assembly is also fitted with a carrying handle and wind around hose stowage. The air cylinder is charged to 207 bar with clean,dry air from the ships breathing air charging panel, if fitted, or from the ships usual charging facilities ashore and will charge an SPE to 10 bar.
**Note.**   In the event that an SPE is overcharged, especially when using this method, the excess pressure should be released by standing the SPE upright and depressing the valve stem inside the air charging connection (Schraeder valve).

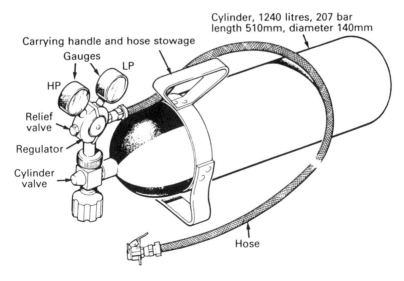

Cylinder, 1240 litres, 207 bar
length 510mm, diameter 140mm

Carrying handle and hose stowage

Gauges

LP

HP

Relief valve

Regulator

Cylinder valve

Hose

**Figure 5.3   Portable air charging equipment**

**0505. Foot pump.** In an emergency the SPE(AFFF) may be charged using a foot pump. The method of charging is self evident in that the pump discharge hose is connected direct to the SPE charging connection. The pressure to be achieved in the SPE is 7 bar.

**0506. Stored pressure extinguisher (dry powder) (SPE(DP))**
This extinguisher is provided near to, or in, the accesses to some machinery spaces, in the flight deck area and in hangars for fighting liquid fuel fires. It is especially useful for fighting liquid fuelled pressure spray fires.
The discharge from this appliance can be controlled by means of the operating lever which can be released whilst it is redirected, thus preventing wastage. It must be pressurized to 10 bar with DRY air from the portable charging assembly.

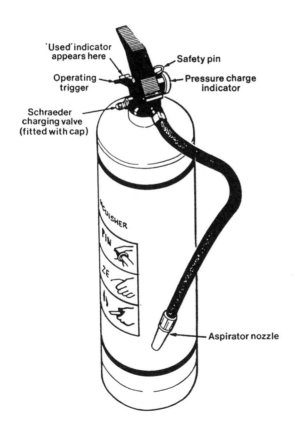

Figure 5.4    9 litre SPE (dry powder) - SPE(DP)

**0507.  SPE(DP) filling.** The SPE(DP) should be recharged with dry powder in a dry compartment as follows:

a.   Ensure the extinguisher is fully discharged

b.   Remove the discharge head assembly, clean of all powder residues with a soft brush.

c.   Clean the Schraeder valve assembly, if necessary removing the valve core.

d.   Clean out the cylinder using a soft brush ensuring the inside of the cylinder is dry.  Particular attention is to be paid to the threads and joint sealing faces.

e.   Using a suitable chute as a funnel pour the contents of one 25lb bag of powder into the cylinder.

f.   Check cleanliness and absence of powder from the screw threads and joint faces, then re-fit the head assembly.

g.   Pressurise with DRY air, via the Schraeder valve, to 10 bar.

   **Note.** Do not use a foot pump in this (the SPE(DP)) application.

**0508.  CO2 fire extinguisher 2kg.** (*see* paragraph 0603.a)

<u>Warning:</u>    When operating CO2 fire extinguishers hold only by the operating handle and any thermally insulated grip on the nozzle.  Holding the cylinder or the horn may well cause ice 'burns'.

   a.    CO2 fire extinguishers provided in compartments containing high voltage electrical equipment are fitted with a flexible hose and plug, which fits an inlet socket on the electronic cabinets.

   b.    For use on open equipment and elsewhere in these compartments the hose is fitted with a hand applicator, which fits over the plug, designed to prevent hand contact with the end of the hose (*see* Figure 5.5).

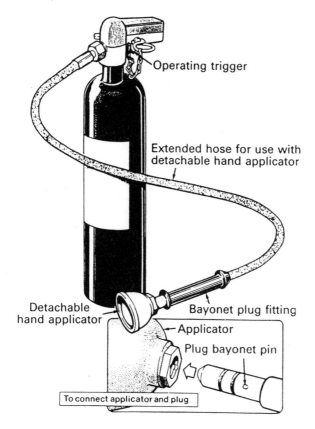

Figure 5.5  CO2 fire extinguisher

c. Elsewhere in the ship CO2 fire extinguishers fitted with a rigid horn are supplied for dealing with electrical fires. (*see* Figure 5.6)

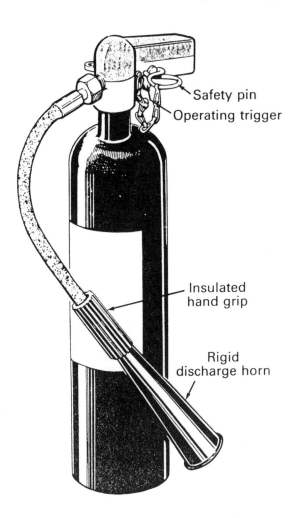

Safety pin

Operating trigger

Insulated hand grip

Rigid discharge horn

**Figure 5.6  CO2 fire extinguisher with rigid discharge horn**

d.   CO2 fire extinguishers cannot be recharged onboard.   When discharged, or partially discharged, they are to be returned through naval stores for recharging.

**0509. PD25 Dry Powder Extinguisher** (*see also* paragraph **0502**)
This extinguisher (*see* Figure 5.7) is provided near to, or in, the accesses to some machinery spaces and on flight deck areas and in hangars for fighting liquid fuel fires, and is especially useful for fighting liquid fuelled pressure spray fires (*see* paragraph **0602**). After use these extinguishers must be refilled in a dry atmosphere and a new $CO_2$ pressurizing charge fitted. It is obsolescent and is being replaced by the SPE(DP).

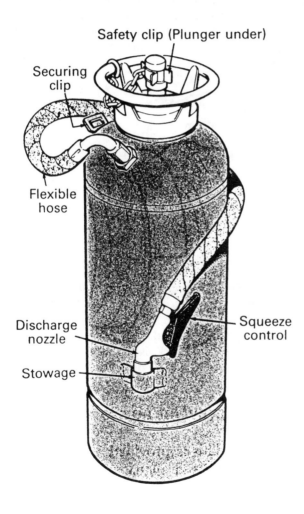

**Figure 5.7 PD25 Dry Powder Extinguisher**

## Nozzles

**0510.**  Two types of nozzle are provided in service:

a.  *Firefighter nozzle.* This is provided at all fire hydrants, in all ships, except on weather decks. It is stowed in the shut position, that is, the rotating sleeve turned fully anti clockwise (looking from the operators end), bringing the rotating sleeve toward the operator. Opening the nozzle by rotating the sleeve clockwise one quarter off a turn produces a waterwall. A further quarter of a turn produces a ragged jet of water to fight the fire. This nozzle has a low water discharge rate and is used for fighting fires.

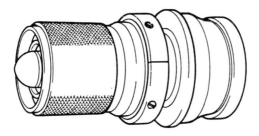

**Figure 5.8 Firefighter nozzle**

b.  *Waterwall nozzle.* This is provided at all weatherdeck hydrants and three are kept in each FRP fire locker for use in providing waterwalls. It is stowed in the shut position which is achieved by turning the rotating sleeve clockwise (looking from the operator) which brings the rotating sleeve towards the operator. Opening the nozzle by rotating the sleeve anti clockwise produces, initially, a jet, but the nozzle must be opened fully to produce the desired waterwall.

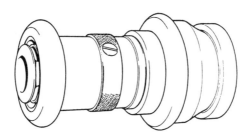

**Figure 5.9  Waterwall nozzle**

**0511. Hose couplings.** Firefighting hoses are joined together and connected to the HPSW main by instantaneous couplings. Each hose has a male coupling at one end and a female at the other. All hydrants have female connections so that, when coupling up to a hose the male end of the hose must be taken to the hydrant  and the female end towards the fire.

**0512. Stowage and care of hoses.** A hose should, at all times, be coupled to each hydrant and a (shut) nozzle connected so that water can be delivered immediately when it is required. Although hoses are fairly robust they need care if they are to be kept in good order, and the following instructions must be observed:

   a.   Hoses are to be faked out in their stowages ready for running out (*see* Figure 5.10). Where double hose baskets are fitted  the hose in the section of the basket closest to the bulkhead must be faked and the hose in the basket furthest from the bulkhead rolled.

   b.   Charged hoses should not be dragged over rough surfaces, especially when kinked.

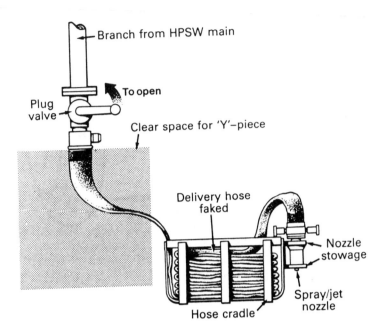

**Figure 5.10  Stowage of hoses**

c.  Hoses may chafe (due to vibration) and kink where they first touch
the deck after leaving a portable pump and will also tend to kink
when leaving hydrants.  Arrangements should be made to prevent
kinking, which reduces water flow, and to protect hoses from chafing
by wrapping rags round the hose at the deck contact point,  Similarly,
protective padding should be used where hoses pass over sharp edges
such as watertight door of hatch coamings.

d.  To avoid subjecting hoses to sudden shock or strain, hydrants and
pump delivery valves should always be opened slowly.  The sudden
closure of nozzles should be avoided.

e.  Hoses must be drained and wiped down before re-stowing.  To expel
water the hoses must be under-run at shoulder height.  When re-
stowing the position  or the previous folds should be shifted and the
nozzles turned to the shut position (*see* paragraph **0510**).

f.    Hoses should be washed and flushed after contamination with fuels, oils, greases, and after use with AFFF.

**0513.    Foam producing appliances.**    These consist of foam making branchpipes, the FB5(X) Mks 1 and 2, the FB10(X) and the FB10/10 (a commercial replacement for the FB10(X)), the inline inductors FBU(X)5 and FBU10(X) (fitted only in or near hangars) and the centre feed hose-reel (CFHR), details of which are as follows.

a.    The **FB5(X)** is a lightweight foam making branchpipe for general use against liquid fuel fires (except in the hangar or an the flight deck where the larger FB10(X)/FB10/10  is used).  The pick up assembly (suction hose and spill) is connected by a quick release coupling.  To induce AFFF the cap must be removed from the 20 litre container and the spill inserted.  This drill is repeated using back up containers as the previous container empties.  This branch pipe will also put foam into machinery spaces via the foam inlet tubes.  The FB5(X) should only be used with No.2 hoses (No.1 hoses restrict the flow rate and are susceptible to kinking).  One drum of foam lasts approximately 1 minute.

b.    The **FB5(X) Mk.2** has an on/off  facility which allows the hose to be fully charged but the flow shut off at the nozzle.  A non return valve in the pick up spill prevents water flowing back into the AFFF drum. The Mk.2 is also fitted with a foam mix selector which, for RN use, must be pinned at the 6% AFFF position.

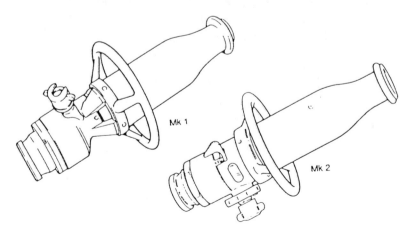

**Figure 5.11  Foam making branchpipes FB5(X) Mks 1 and 2**

c.   The *FB(10)X foam making branchpipe* (*see* Figure 5.12)and its
     successor the **FB10/10** (which is a commercial variant, similar in
     appearance and performance to  the FB10(X)) are high output
     branchpipes used at helicopter landing positions, on flightdecks and
     on vehicle decks. Hydrants at these positions have an inline inductor
     (the FBU10(X)) bolted to the flange before  the instantaneous
     coupling. The pick-up assembly is attached to the inductor and has
     a shut off cock. The inductor passes the mixture of AFFF and water
     through the hose to the branchpipe which aerates and delivers the
     foam. To produce foam of good quality the FB(10)X needs HPSW
     mains pressure of at least 4.2 bar. This branchpipe can deliver foam
     to a distance in the form of a jet, or less forcibly as a spray.

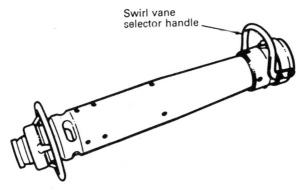

Swirl vane
selector handle

**Figure 5.12   FB(10)X foam making branchpipe**

**0514. Portable inline inductor (FBU5(X)).** This inductor (*see* Figure 5.13)
is designed for use with the FB5(X). Its purpose is to allow AFFF to be
introduced into the hoseline at, or near, the hydrant position and not directly
into the branchpipe. This allows the operator much greater mobility in that
he is no longer constrained by the AFFF containers and the pick up
assembly, especially when passing through WT openings or using ladders.
The inline inductor has a stowage bracket with a 1.8 m length of No.1 hose
(for use between the hydrant and the inductor). The pickup spill for the
inductor is taken from the FB5(X), which no longer needs it when being
used in conjunction with the inline inductor. The spill connecting point on
the FB5(X) need not be blanked off.  The inline inductor should not be
used when the FB5(X) is being used to introduce foam via foam inlet tubes.
They are best kept for use with firefighting hoses which are being moved
around by operators, as opposed to static hoses, e.g., those led to foam inlet
tubes.

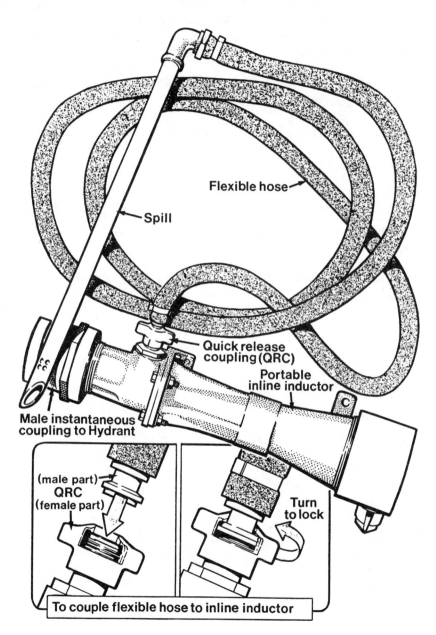

Figure 5.13 Portable inline inductor - (FBU5(X))

**0515.   Centre feed hose-reel (CFHR).**   This is a first aid firefighting appliance, normally used in the FOAM mode, but with the facility to be used in the WATER mode for boundary cooling.  It is normally left in the STANDBY condition with:

a.  The high pressure salt water isolating valve (if fitted) pinned or wired in the OPEN position.

b.  The 3 position selector valve on the inductor set to the OFF position.

c.  The nozzle valve on the hose end set to the OFF position.

### Notes

1.  A copy of the operating instructions and a deck plan of compartments served should be posted adjacent to every hose-reel  assembly.

2.  The FOAM (F) and WATER (W) positions of the valve and the outboard end of the operating handle are to be marked with photoluminescent paint.

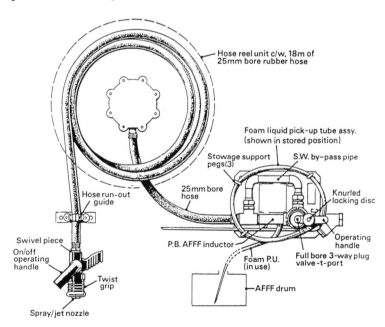

**Figure 5.14  Centre feed (foam/water)  hose-reel unit**

# 6  Firefighting tactics and techniques

At all times personnel and equipment must be organized so that the attack on a fire will be immediate, continuous and aggressive.

## Use of first aid firefighting appliances

0601.  Solid fires.  Solid fires are to be attacked using either the centre feed hose-reel (CFHR) using its AFFF inductor or a 9 litre stored pressure extinguisher (AFFF), (SPE(AFFF)).  These appliances are to be used as follows:

a.  CENTRE FEED HOSE REEL OPERATING INSTRUCTIONS

**First aid firefighters.** The FOAM mode is to be used for all first aid firefighting operations with this equipment.

1.  Remove the cap from the AFFF drum and insert the spill pick up.

2.  Select the FOAM position on the selector valve.

3.  Proceed to the location of the fire.

4.  Direct the nozzle away from the fire and open the nozzle valve.

5.  When foam is being produced attack the fire.

6.  The next man on the scene must re-supply AFFF.

**Boundary cooling.**  The WATER mode is to be used when boundary cooling.

1.  Select WATER position on the selector valve.

2.  Proceed to the location requiring boundary cooling.

3.  Open the nozzle and select ragged spray.

4.  Boundary cool using the minimum amount of water.

b.  *9 litre SPE(AFFF)* (*see* Figures 5.1 and 5.2).  Remove from its stowage and check that the gauge indicates an adequate charge. Holding the appliance in front of the body, approach the fire keeping as low as possible. When in a safe discharging position (with a clear withdrawal route), and as close to the fire as possible, free the hose, pull out the safety pin and direct the nozzle over the fire beating the flames down. Then direct the discharge to the heart of the flames, breaking open the combustibles as much as possible. A SPE charged to a pressure of 10 bar will give a maximum throw of 7.5m and last for approximately 50 seconds. An SPE charged to 7 bar will give a maximum throw of 6.5m and lasts approximately 40 seconds.

**0602. Oil fires.** Oil fires are attacked, in the first instance, as described in paragraph **0601,** except where dry powder extinguishers are more appropriate and available (some machinery space accesses and on flight decks and in hangars) especially on liquid fuel fires which are under pressure and producing a spray. Dry powder extinguishers are used as follows.

a.  *PD25 dry powder extinguisher* (now obsolescent). It should be used as close to the fire as possible and certainly within 6 metres. It is operated by removing the safety clip and then striking the plunger, holding it upright whilst squeezing the trigger and employing a sweeping, horizontal motion with the nozzle directed at the base of the fire . A continuous discharge lasts between 35-40 seconds but after 20 seconds the knock down effect reduces.

b.  *9 Kg stored pressure extinguisher (Dry powder)(SPE(DP)).* This extinguisher is similar in appearance and operation to the SPE(AFFF), the difference being that its instruction legend is in blue (instead of red) and with 1" wide blue bands around the extinguisher body, above and below the legend, (*see* Figure 5.6a). It is operated in the same manner as the SPE(AFFF) by removing the safety pin and checking that ten bar is registered on the gauge, press the trigger and employ a sweeping horizontal motion with the nozzle directed at the base of the fire. *A continuous discharge lasts for approximately 20 seconds.*

**0603. Electrical fires.** Wherever possible the equipment and/or the circuits on fire should be isolated. Delays in achieving this should not prevent the fire from being attacked in the following manner:

a.  Electrical and electronic equipment fires should be attacked using 2 kg $CO_2$ fire extinguishers (*see* Figures 6.4 and 6.5). The extinguisher is operated holding it by the squeeze grip release valve, removing the safety pin and then pressing the trigger of the grip very firmly to ensure full discharge and to avoid 'freezing up' at the orifice. The $CO_2$ discharge should be directed at the base of the fire from as near as possible, ensuring that the insulated handle on the discharge horn is used as the grip (*see* Figure 5.5).

b.  Other electrical fires can be attacked using AFFF first aid appliances (SPE or CFHR) before the equipment or circuits have been isolated providing the voltage does not exceed 440V ac or 800V dc, and the appliance is at least 1.8m from the power source.

**Note** In the event of minor fire symptoms being noticed, e.g., wisps of smoke coming from electronic equipment, switchboards, etc., switching of the power supply may be sufficient to cause these symptoms to disappear. Discretion is therefore necessary in initial firefighting action. Wherever possible electrical fires should be fought using $CO_2$ gas.

**0604.  Ventilation control.** In the event of fire the local starters to ventilation systems, which are not controlled by breakers, should be tripped. These systems may be re-started on the authority of HQ1. Ventilation controlled by switchboards/SCC/HQ1 is crash stopped and then controlled in accordance with ship's orders.

**Note** ACU's fitted to individual compartments (and for that compartment only) and full recirculation ATU systems for unmanned spaces, should not be stopped.

**0605. Smoke control.** A smoke boundary can be set up by closing appropriate doors, hatches, ventilation flaps and valves and, most importantly, the fitted smoke curtains which are also used to provide access and exit from the fire zone. Remember, under some circumstances the ventilation systems can be used to remove or contain smoke.

**0606.  Fire boundary control.** All inflammable material and dangerous items, e.g., compressed gas bottles, chemicals, etc., should be removed from the compartments adjoining the fire boundary to safer areas.

**0607. Fire boundary cooling.** Once the fire boundary has been established, arrangements should be made to prevent the conduction of heat via bulkheads, decks and trunkings and so contain the spread of the fire. This is achieved as follows.

a.  Bulkhead and deckhead linings on the fire boundary should be removed, or access gained through them, in order to allow the cooling spray to reach the heated structure.

b.  Apply the minimum amount of cooling water sufficient to keep the plating moist.

c.  Never leave cooling appliances unattended.

d.  Prevent the accumulation of free surface water. It should be pumped overboard or drained to the lowest, smallest, watertight compartment possible.

e.  To prevent boundary cooling compartments becoming untenable, use exhaust ventilation (with HQ1/SCC permission) to remove steam.

f.  Cover electrical equipment on the cooling boundary, using plastic sheet (polyamide, Nylon 6, transparent protective film) to protect it from water. Switch off high voltage electrical equipment sited on the cooling boundary (with HQ1/SCC) permission).

**Fire approach technique**
**0608.** Sometimes the position of the fire and the layout of the ship dictate that only one method of approach is practicable on order to attack it. Whenever there is a choice, the methods preferred are in the following order:

a.  *Approach from the same level.* This is the preferred route to any fire as the firefighting equipment is easier to handle and access/exit is more convenient.

   (1)  Solid fuel fire - *see* Figure 6.1

   (2)  Oil fuel fire (diesel, hydraulic oil, etc.) - *see* Figure 6.3 (which illustrates a four man team, with an FB5(X) instead of the Firefighter nozzle, and an extra man, No.5, on the waterwall), and adapt this drill to suit an entry via a door (*see* Figure 6.1)

b.   *Approach from above.* The firefighters will encounter a smoke/heat layer which deters all but the most experienced and determined firefighters. Invariably access to the fire is gained via a hatch as follows:

(1)   Solid fuel fire - *see* Figure 6.2.

(2)   Oil fuel fire (diesel, hydraulic oil, etc.) - *see* Figure 6.3.

c.   *Approach from below.* This is the coolest and most smoke free route to a fire but is rarely available on a ship. Difficulties will be experienced opening hatches above in order to access the fire area. It is an energy consuming and difficult approach which is compensated for by lack of smoke, lower temperature and the fact that, once the hatch is opened, water or foam can be bounced off the deckhead or bulkheads towards the seat of the fire.

**0609. Premature withdrawal of firefighters.** Should the warning whistle on the BA of a member of the firefighting team sound:

a.   prematurely, namely before the pressure gauge indicates 7 minutes of air remaining in the set; or

b.   when 7 minutes of air are indicated in the set and the relief firefighting team has not arrived; or

one or more of the firefighting team has to withdraw due to injury or some unforeseen circumstance, then this is to be communicated to the FRP (allowing whoever is in charge of the firefighting teams to make arrangements for timely relief) and the entire team must withdraw ensuring minimal support for the fire, e.g. closing doors and hatches behind them. The relief team will then recommence the attack on the fire using the appropriate procedures for opening doors and hatches. **Wherever possible the attack on the fire must be maintained continuously and aggressively.**

**0610. Fire sentries.** When a fire has occurred and has been extinguished an appropriate number of suitably briefed sentries must be posted in order to deal with, and raise the alarm in the event of re-ignition.

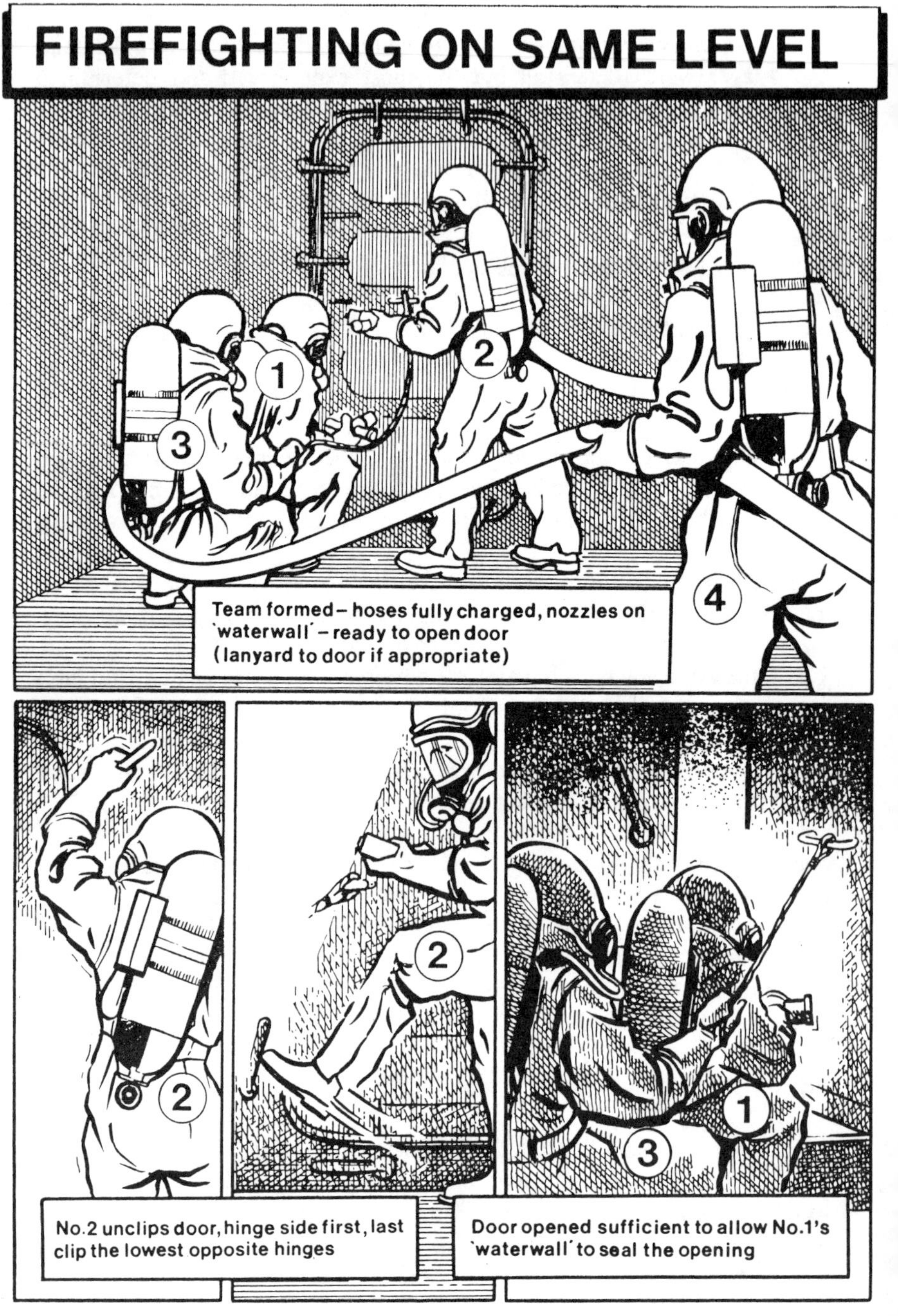

Fig. 6.1  Firefighting on the same level

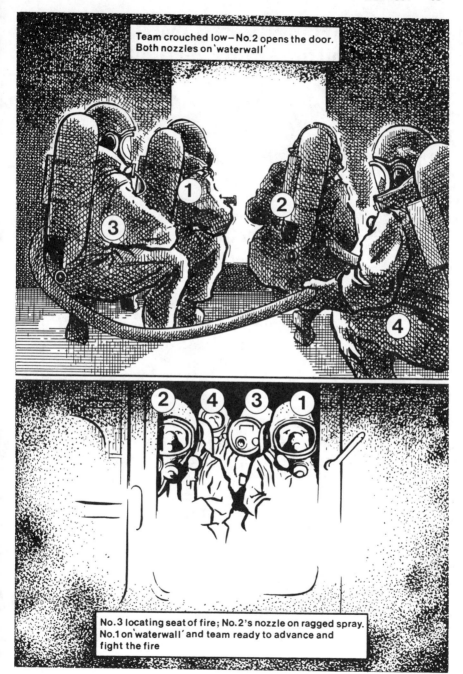

Fig. 6.1 Firefighting on the same level (continued)

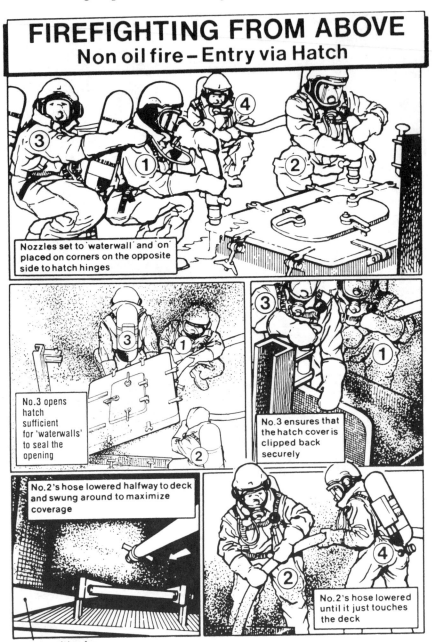

Fig. 6.2   Firefighting from above.

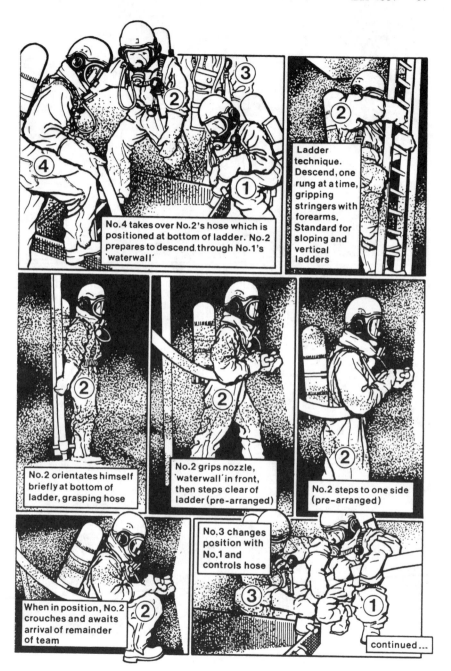

Fig. 6.2 Firefighting from above (continued)

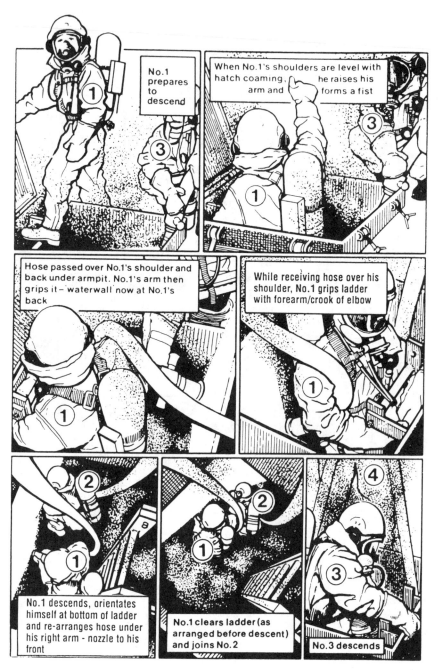

**Fig. 6.2 Firefighting from above (continued)**

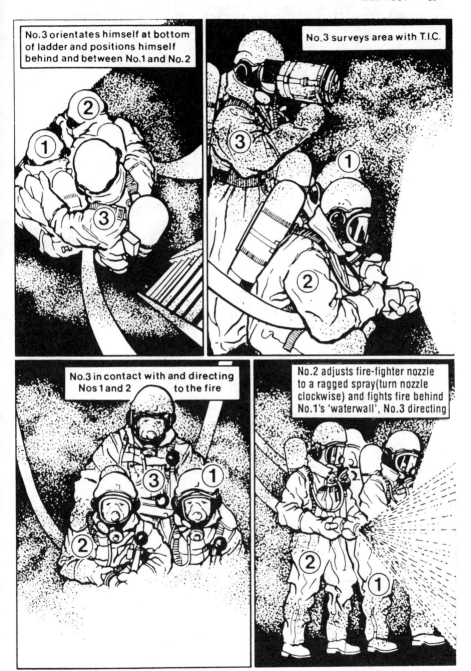

Fig. 6.2 Firefighting from above  (continued)

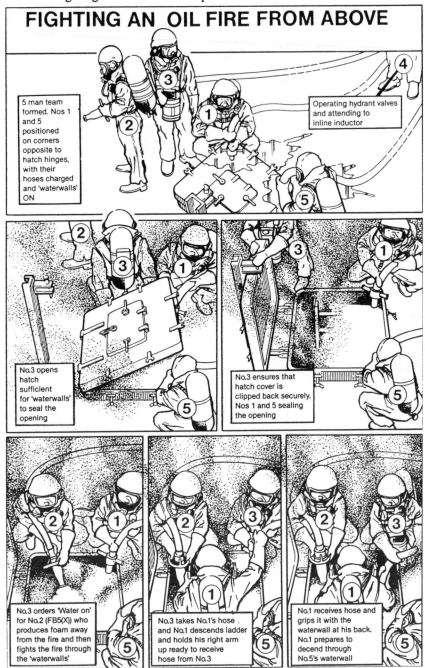

Fig. 6.3 Firefighting an oil fire from above.

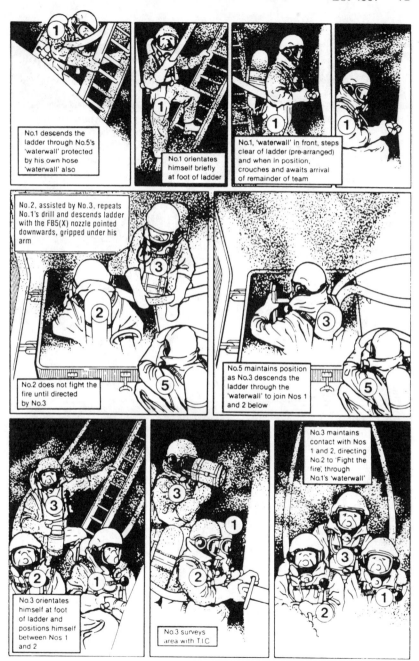

**Fig. 6.3 Firefighting an oil fire from above (continued).**

Fig 6.4 Submarine firefighting on same level - 3 man team with CFHR

Fig 6.5 Submarine firefighting on same level - 3 man team with FB5X

**Fig 6.6 Submarine firefighting from above - 3 man team with 5BX**

Fig 6.6 Submarine firefighting from above - 3 man with 5BX (continued)

**Fig 6.7 Submarine firefighting from above - 3 man with CFHR**

**Fig 6.7 Submarine firefighting from above - 3 man CFHR (continued)**

**Fig 6.8 Submarine firefighting from below - 2 man with CFHR**

Fig 6.8 Submarine firefighting from below - 2 man with CFHR (continued)

# 7  Personal protection

**0701. Introduction.** Firefighting personnel need to be protected, as far as is possible, against the effects off:

- heat;

- toxic gases or lack of oxygen;

- loss of vision;

- loss of communication;

- physical damage, especially to the head.

This is achieved by wearing the protective clothing and equipment that comprises the full firefighting rig.

**Protective clothing - general**

**0702. Basic firefighting rig.** This consists of Proban treated cotton No.8's, or cotton overall's, DMS boots, cotton underwear and woollen socks. When engaged in firefighting operations collars should be buttoned up and the sleeves rolled down and cuffs buttoned. *Nylon clothing must not be worn by firefighters.*

**0703. Full firefighting rig.** This consists of basic firefighting rig plus anti-flash hood and gloves, Fearnought suit and fearnought mittens, seamen's stockings, firefighting boots, BA and bulb horn, slim tank helmet (with caplamp) and portable radio transceiver. (*see* Figures 7.1 & 7.2.)

### Note

1.  When wearing the above remember to occasionally shrug within the clothing and move the tight spots. This will allow the air enclosed to circulate more freely and improve comfort.

2.  Remember that when your ears start to tingle it is a warning of rise in body temperature and that steps should be taken to vacate the area quickly. Too long an exposure to a great heat will induct heat exhaustion and sudden collapse.

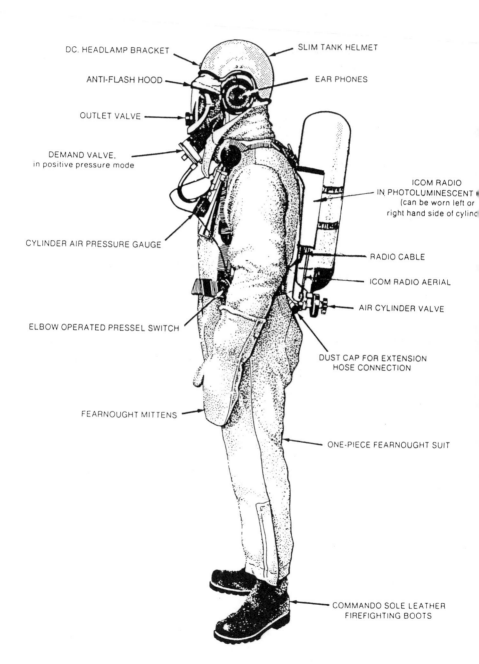

**Fig. 7.1 Full firefighting rig (left view)**

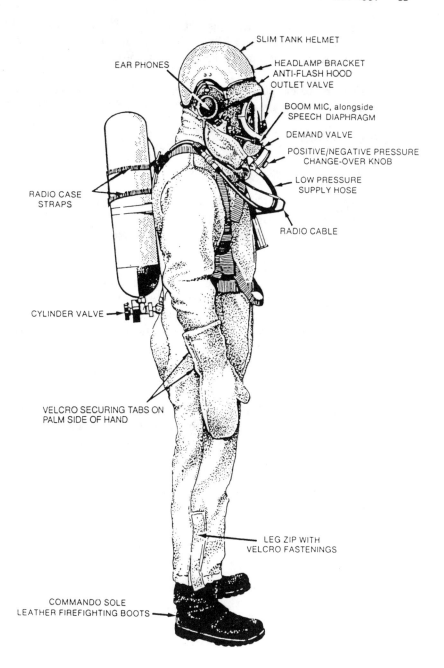

SLIM TANK HELMET

EAR PHONES

HEADLAMP BRACKET
ANTI-FLASH HOOD
OUTLET VALVE

BOOM MIC, alongside
SPEECH DIAPHRAGM

DEMAND VALVE

POSITIVE/NEGATIVE PRESSURE
CHANGE-OVER KNOB

LOW PRESSURE
SUPPLY HOSE

RADIO CASE
STRAPS

RADIO CABLE

CYLINDER VALVE

VELCRO SECURING TABS ON
PALM SIDE OF HAND

LEG ZIP WITH
VELCRO FASTENINGS

COMMANDO SOLE
LEATHER FIREFIGHTING BOOTS

**Fig.7.2  Full firefighting rig (right view)**

3.  If a fearnought suit becomes wet the heat will cause steam to be produced and the wearer will risk injury from scalding. Once a suit has been wetted it must be kept moist (to protect the wearer).

4.  All items of clothing and equipment needed to complete the full firefighting rig are stowed in the FRP locker, BA locker and nearby.

**Full firefighting rig**

**0704.  Clothing.** (*see* Figures 7.1 & 7.2)

a.  *Firefighting boots.* The firefighting boots are leather high leg boots, with a thick commando style sole, re-enforced toe cap and heel with two loops at the top making them easier to pull on.

b.  *Anti-flash hood and gloves.* Ready use anti-flash hood and gloves are to be stowed in each BASCCA locker. The hood is worn with its mantle tucked inside the collar of the shirt or overalls. When wearing BA the chin bag of the hood is to be tucked over the equalization valve below the chin of the facemask. Anti- flash must be kept clean and white to provide the designed level of protection. It must not be marked in any way e. g. felt tipped pen or paint. If necessary a second hood may be worn to give greater protection.

c.  *One piece Fearnought coveralls. (Zirpro treated).* These incorporate a zip fastener from the left knee to the right shoulder and another zip at the bottom of each leg, to facilitate the dressing procedure.

d.  *Fearnought mittens (Zirpro treated).* These are worn over the top of the cuff of the fearnought suit with the Velcro fasteners on the inside of the wrist.

**0705. Breathing apparatus - general** (*see* Figures 7.1 & 7.2.)

a.   Breathing apparatus, Self Contained, Compressed Air (Damage Control and Firefighting) (BASCCA(DC&FF) are stowed in lockers which are painted red with BASCCA(DC&FF) in white lettering. These are sited near FRPP's, upper deck fire re-entry posts and in pairs in lobbies and airlocks off the weather decks. (*see* paragraphs **0709/13.**) A non-magnetic version of BASCCA (DC&FF) is supplied in some MCMV's

b.   The safety control equipment (BA control board, personal line, BA control armband and bulbhorn) is to be stowed in the BA locker. Guidelines are stowed in the four BA lockers adjacent to the FRPP and also in the upper deck re-entry locker.

c.   The use of equipments in a search and rescue (SAR) is detailed in BR 2170(1) paragraphs 2259-67.

d.   Smoke mask assemblies are provided in all ships. Although their prime task is for allowing safe entry into foul air compartments they do have a firefighting capability - when BASCCA's are not available or appropriate. Smoke masks are also useful for post fire, or toxic environment, sentries. When in use the operator draws air from the same space as that used by the holder of the air inlet filter (*see* Figure 7.3). The holder must ensure that his own exhaled breath is not drawn into the filter. Users need to be strong and determined. The maximum length of the hose is 27 metres.

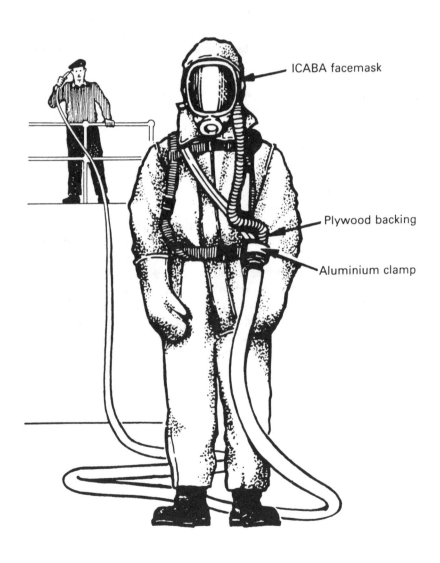

**Figure 7.3  Smoke mask**

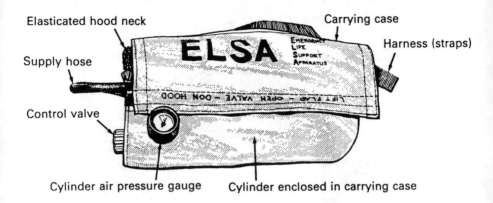

**Figure 7.4  Emergency Life Support Apparatus (ELSA)**

   e.   Emergency Life Support Apparatus (ELSA) is to be used only for escape from, or through, smoke logged compartments.  ELSA is not to be used for firefighting or damage control work.

**0706.  Thermal Imaging Camera (TIC) - general** (*see* Figures 5.5 to 5.7). TIC's are used by the leaders (No.3) of the four man firefighting teams. However, if they were required, they may previously have been used by the attack party.

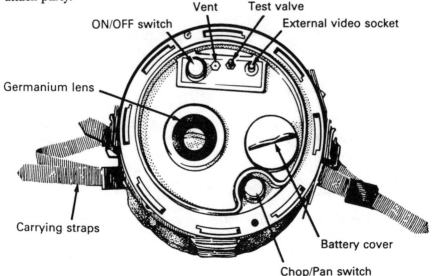

**Figure 7.5  Thermal Imaging Camera**

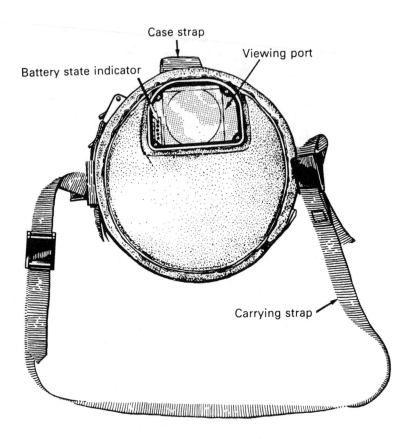

**Figure 7.6    Thermal Imaging Camera**

a.  TIC's (large or miniaturized) are to be stowed at FRP/section bases, or nearby, in secure stowages which are readily accessible in an emergency.

b.  The large TIC must have its visor fitted before use.

c.  Ni-cad rechargeable batteries are to be used for training purposes (duration approximately 45 minutes) and Duracell MN1500 batteries (duration approximately 90 minutes) are to be fitted before use in an emergency.

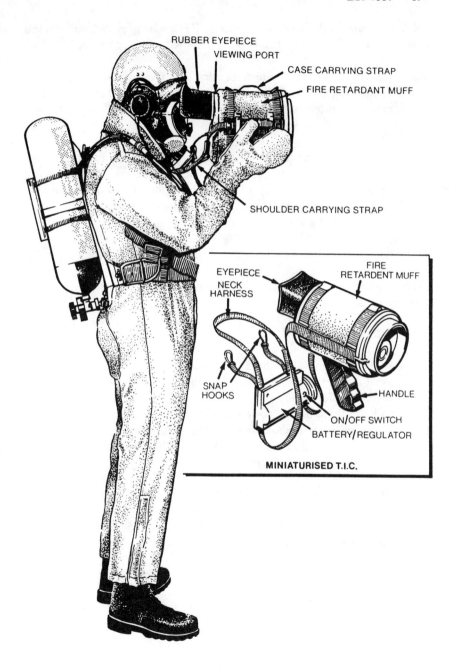

Figure 7.7 Thermal Imaging Camera

**0707. Communications - general.** Each FRP will be provided with ten sets (for 2 x 4 men firefighting teams, 1 for the FRP and 1 spare) of:

    a.    portable radio transmitter/receivers (transceivers) (*see* Figure 7.9), comprising a radio body and battery section enclosed in a waterproof case and fitted with a flexible antenna. They are supplied with instructional manuals, and

    b.    slim tank helmets (STH) (*see* Figure 7.8) fitted with an integral dual sided ear shells, a boom microphone, attachment   sockets, and a press-to-speak (pressel) switch with a push in connector to the portable transceiver. There is an attachment for a DC caplamp (*see* Figures 7.1, 7.2 and 7.8).

These items are to be placed together in a secure locker which is readily accessible in an emergency. Where this is not possible the transceivers are to be stowed in the FRP lockers and the slim tank helmets stowed, in their carrying bags, nearby.

**0708. Safety equipment.**

    a.    A distress signal (bulb horn), an armband and BA control board are stowed with the BA in its locker. During firefighting operations the BA controller retains the armband from each set under his control and also operates the BA control board. *A maximum of 8 sets may be controlled by each controller.* The bulb horn, worn by each fire fighter is clipped to the plastic D ring of the BA harness on the left hand side of the chest (*see* Figure 7.1).

    b.    Guide lines are stowed in BASCCA lockers adjacent to FRP and FP posts (including upper deck re-entry FPP.). Personal lines are attached to each BASCCA. Both are to be used as directed by whoever is in charge of SAR teams during SAR operations (*see* BR 2170(1), paragraphs 2259-2268).

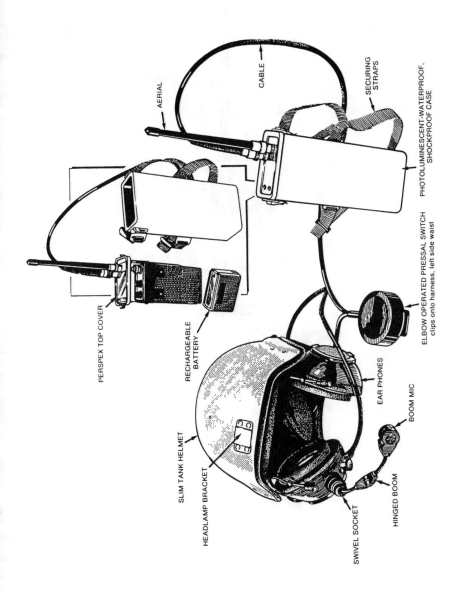

**Figure 7.8  Slim tank helmet kit**

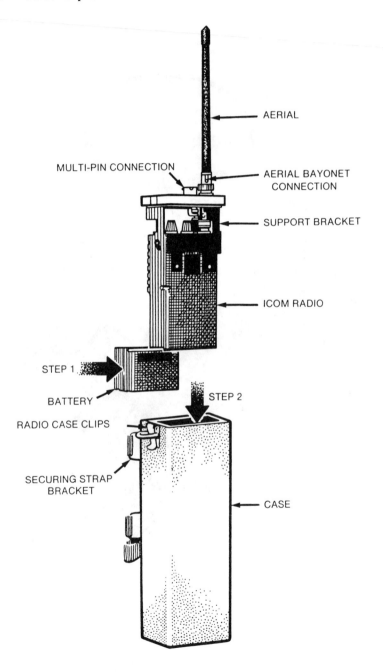

**Figure 7.9  Radio transceiver**

# Breathing apparatus, self contained, compressed air (DC&FF)

0709.  Components

    a.  Facemask assembly.

    b.  Frame and harness assembly.

    c.  Air cylinder and valve assembly.

    d.  High pressure reducing valve.

    e.  Warning whistle.

    f.  Pressure gauge

**0710. Stowage.** This equipment is stowed in bulkhead mounted lockers (*see* paragraph 0704.a) together with an anti-flash hood and gloves. A tally detailing the functional and face seal checks is attached to the inside of the door. The door can be removed to prevent obstruction.

**0711. Description.** The BASCCA (DC&FF) has a face mask assembly fitted with an ori-nasal mask, exhalation valve and demand valve assemblies. The demand valve is designed to permit the use of the apparatus as a positive pressure set for normal operations, so ensuring that any leaks in the face seal are outwards. The frame comprises a backplate with harness attachments and cylinder cradles, with a free air cylinder of 1400 litres capacity at a maximum working pressure of 207 bar. When fully charged the set gives a nominal endurance to the whistle sounding of 27 minutes (*but see* a. & b. below), with a warning whistle set to sound when the duration of the set is reduced to 7 minutes. The pressure at which the whistle should sound is indicated on the pressure gauge by the red coloured segment. This covers the reserve period of 43 bar to zero (7 minutes).

    a.  When BASCCA is worn the wearer must try to control his breathing so that it is rhythmic and steady. Breathing fast, or panting will greatly reduce the wear time.

b. Whenever possible it must be arranged that men with beards are not required to BASCCA(DC&FF) operationally as this reduces the endurance. In wartime all beard are to be shaved off.

c. Remember not to over tighten the facemask harness straps, and that all the air connections are designed to be hand tight.

**0712. Extension equipment.** This comprises:

- a 2 metre extension hose.

- a facemask assembly and harness; and

- a 20 metre extension hose

These items are stowed in a red painted locker which has a drop down door. The tally on the outside of the door reads EXTENSION EQUIPMENT FOR BASCCA (DC&FF), the tally on the inside gives the operating instructions.

## Operating the BASCCA (DC&FF)

**0713. Donning/functional check.** The operator, assisted by his controller, should don the apparatus as follows;

a. Remove the facemask from its stowage clip and place the neck strap over the head so allowing the facemask to hang on the chest. The neck strap must always be outside the operator's clothing and not in contact with the skin.

b. Release the apparatus securing bands and pass the right arm through the right shoulder strap; lift the apparatus clear of the locker and pass the left arm though the left shoulder strap.

c. Adjust the shoulder straps by pulling backwards towards the cylinder, then fasten the waist belt and chest strap. Do not over tighten the shoulder straps otherwise the waist belt may be too high.

d. Select negative pressure mode using the change over knob (*see* paragraph **0714** note 2).

e.    Open the cylinder valve fully.  The warning whistle should sound briefly.  If the whistle is not heard then shut the valve , select positive pressure mode and reduce pressure in the HP air hose to 43 bar.  If the whistle still does not operate it is defective and this fact must be reported to the BA co-ordinator

f.    Select negative pressure mode and then open the cylinder valve. Should the air then leak from the demand valve the apparatus is faulty and must not be used. The BA co-ordinator is to be informed.

g.    The BA controller removes and retains the control armband and records the set number and the operator's name on the control board.

**0714.  Face seal checks.**  When the operator is required to commence his task the following checks are to be carried out:

a.    Don the facemask and, when it is fully adjusted for correct fitting, select the positive pressure mode (*see* note 2) and then commence to breathe from the apparatus. Ensure that the head harness is central at the top/back of the head by first adjusting the two lower straps at the same time and then the two upper straps.

b.    Breathe deeply to ensure that the demand and exhalation valves are working correctly.

c.    Observe the pressure gauge; close the cylinder valve and then open it half a turn, take and hold, a deep breath; then close the valve. Check that the pressure gauge reading does not drop by more than 5 bar in 10 seconds. Open the cylinder valve fully.

d.    Check that the bulb horn works. It is only to be used for signalling an emergency.

### Note

The facemask sealing check is to be carried out whenever an operator dons the facemask for operational purposes.

## Breathing apparatus control

**0715.** When the BA's are used operationally a control number must be detailed. The BA controller must be well trained in the use of the apparatus and understand the important part he plays in the safety arrangements for the firefighters in the fire zone. He must always be in possession of a reliable timepiece and chinagraph pencils.

**0716.** The BA controller must remain outside the fire zone, near to the smoke boundary, and must on no account be detailed for any other duties. He may act as the controller for up to eight men (two four men teams), if they are carrying out the same task, but where possible the preferred number is four.

**0717.** The duties of a breathing apparatus controller are as follows:

a.    Wear all the armbands of the BA's he is controlling

b.    Assist the operator(s) to don and adjust their BA and to carry out functional and face seal checks (*see* paragraphs **0713/14**).

c.    Mark up the control board (Form S3047)(*see* paragraph **0718**).

d.    When its use is directed secure the tail of the guide line to convenient anchorage at the point of entry to the fire zone or incident.

e.    Keep a sharp listening watch for any distress signals from the bulb horns.

f.    Ensure that the BA controller of the relief firefighting team and the rating i/c of the support party are informed of the time the relief team should enter the fire zone in order to relieve the previous team.

g.    Inform the officer or rating in charge where an operator has not returned at his *time due out*.

h.    Tend the apparatus when it is used in conjunction with a 20 metre extension hose and facemask.

i.    When controlling an operator, who is using the 20 metre extension hose, use and agreed signal to recall him.

j.    Replace the control armbands over the pressure gauges when the operators report back from the fire zone/incident area.

**0718.  Completion of control board (Form S3047).** The BA controller carries out the following instructions after the firefighting team has been briefed by the officer/rating i/c of firefighting.

a.    Complete columns A and B of the control board whilst firefighters are dressing and before the briefing, if possible.

b.    When the facemasks are donned and the operators commence breathing, the remainder of the of the control board is to be completed (*see* Figure 7.10). All control board instructions must be carried out before the operators enter the fire zone/incident area

c.    When the operators return from the task, the BA controller must carry out the exit instructions as detailed on the control board.

d.    When the operators return from the task they remove their facemasks with the change-over knob set to the negative pressure mode.

e.    If re-entry to the fire zone/incident area is required, the operator and his BA controller must check the remaining cylinder pressure and complete the control board as instructed in a and b. He must also carry out the faceseal check.

## Control board for BASCCA (DCFF) 207 bar working pressure.

RN Form S3047 (Revised 10/85)

| SET No. | A OPERATOR'S NAME | TASK | B CYLINDER PRESSURE (bar) | C TIME TO WHISTLE (min) | D TIME STARTED TO BREATHE | E TIME RELIEF DUE IN | F TIME RETURN COMMENCES | G TIME DUE OUT |
|---|---|---|---|---|---|---|---|---|
| 1 | KEATING S. F/F No 2 | | 207 | 27 | 1200 | 1220 | 1227 | 1234 |
| 27 | ADAMS T | " 1 | 200 | 25 | 1200 | 1218 | 1225 | 1232 |
| 13 | HOBDAY | " 4 | 195 | 25 | 1200 | 1218 | 1225 | 1232 |
| 6 | SMALLEY | " 3 | 185 | 23 | 1200 | 1216 | 1223 | 1230 |
| 8 | SMITH K. F/F No 1 | | 207 | 27 | 1216 | 1236 | 1243 | 1250 |
| 9 | McNAUGHTON | " 2 | 200 | 25 | 1216 | 1234 | 1241 | 1248 |
| 11 | CURTIS J | " 3 | 207 | 27 | 1216 | 1236 | 1243 | 1250 |
| 12 | DENNIS T | " 4 | 207 | 27 | 1216 | 1236 | 1243 | 1250 |

**If operator does not emerge by time due out inform officer in charge firefighters**

### Entry Instructions

1. Remove control armband from set – to be worn by control number
2. Before operator enters complete A, B & D
3. Use Endurance Table to complete C
4. Add C to D to complete F
5. Subtract 7 minutes from F to complete E
6. Add 7 minutes to F to complete G
7. Check that the head harness is central at top/back of head
8. Ensure demand valve is in positive pressure mode
9. Carry out face seal check (pressure drop to be less than 5 bar in 10 seconds)

### Exit Instructions

1. Remove armband and place over pressure gauge tube above clip
2. Operator to be debriefed by officer in charge firefighters then report to B.A. Co-ordinator

### Endurance Table

| PRESSURE (bar) | TIME TO WHISTLE (min) |
|---|---|
| 207 | 27 |
| 195 | 25 |
| 180 | 23 |
| 165 | 20 |
| 150 | 18 |
| 135 | 15 |
| 120 | 13 |

At 43 bar the whistle blows and 7 minutes breathing time remains

Officer in charge firefighters' permission required to START using B.A. if pressure below 170 bars

### Note:

Times are approximate, actual duration will depend on individual and task

Figure 7.10   Breathing Apparatus control board - Form S3047

# Index

Printed in the United Kingdom for HMSO.
Dd 0294721, 4/92, C130, GP 3385/2, CCN 16268.